IMAGES
of America

PENNSYLVANIA
HIGH SCHOOL HOCKEY
CHAMPIONSHIPS

IMAGES
of America

PENNSYLVANIA
HIGH SCHOOL HOCKEY
CHAMPIONSHIPS

Jeff Mauro

ARCADIA
PUBLISHING

Published by Arcadia Publishing
Charleston, South Carolina

Printed in the United States of America

Library of Congress Control Number: 2021935960

For all general information, please contact Arcadia Publishing:
Telephone 843-853-2070
Fax 843-853-0044
E-mail sales@arcadiapublishing.com
For customer service and orders:
Toll-Free 1-888-313-2665

Visit us on the Internet at www.arcadiapublishing.com

*This book is dedicated to the coaches, parents, and players,
present and past, who suit up and give their best to carry
their schools for a chance at the glory of ultimately winning
the Pennsylvania high school hockey championship.*

CONTENTS

ACKNOWLEDGMENTS

It all began in April 1970, when my mother, Mary Mauro, brought me to the Alpine Arena in Swissvale. My older brothers Mike and Fred participated in a hockey game between students from Churchill and Penn Hills, the first high school hockey game in Western Pennsylvania. My love affair with interscholastic hockey began.

In 1975, the idea for schools from across Pennsylvania to compete for one championship came to fruition. Two men who were very influential in making this championship come about were Roger Sharrer and Frank Black. Their passion for the game brought schools together to compete in the very first state championship.

I joined the Western Pennsylvania Interscholastic Hockey League (WPIHL) board of directors in 1995. Folks like Larry Kempert, Ron Steedle, Helen Marrietta, Jay Gamze, Tom Strittmatter, and Bob Knudson were passionate about building high school hockey into the Pennsylvania Interscholastic Hockey League and the Penguins Cup championship.

The Eastern Pennsylvania Interscholastic Hockey Association (EPIHA), including John Graves, Ken Haas, Steve Mescanti, Carl Wood, Greg Dugan, Matt Sacks, and John Povey, are to be commended for building the Flyers Cup into a terrific event now in its 40th year, coveted by high school hockey teams in Eastern Pennsylvania.

In 2000, Kathy Santora completed the monumental task of refurbishing the state championship trophies. Etched in the trophies are the names of the players, coaches, and managers who won state titles. The Pennsylvania high school hockey championship is now in its 45th year.

I had an opportunity to fully appreciate the state championships as a parent. My son Jamie Mauro's Franklin Regional team captured two Penguins Cup championships in 2016 and 2017. The team fell short of its ultimate goal of a state championship in overtime to the seven-time champions Bayard Rustin, coached by Nick Russo.

I would like to personally thank the Pennsylvania hockey community for the streams of pictures and content provided to make this publication a reality.

INTRODUCTION

High school hockey in Pennsylvania was re-established in 1969 in Philadelphia when the Inter-County Scholastic Hockey League (ICSHL) was founded. The league was founded by Marshall Mogiovkin and Kurt Wallin to give more boys the opportunity to play hockey in suburban Philadelphia. Conestoga, O'Hara, Haverford, Swarthmore, Marple Newtown, Malvern Prep, and St. Joseph's were the first programs established in Eastern Pennsylvania. Conestoga won the ICSHL championship in the first three years of play.

The Suburban High School Hockey League (SHSHL) was founded in 1972 with five schools and boasted some of the top programs, including Abington, Archbishop Wood, Council Rock, and Germantown Academy. Abington was the first Philadelphia area school to win a state championship, capturing the Class AA title in 1976 over Gateway High School. The SHSHL has a long history of excellent programs and was led in its inception by league president Andy Richards.

The Lower Bucks County Scholastic Hockey League (LBCSHL) was founded in 1975, playing out of the Grundy Ice Arena in Bristol, Pennsylvania, with seven schools, including Archbishop Ryan, Bishop Egan, and Father Judge, among the charter members.

In 1981, the Eastern High School Hockey League (EHSHL) was founded, playing out of the Haverford Skatium in Havertown, Pennsylvania. The league was founded by Jack Hunt and Mary Cifone to serve the schools on the Main Line of Philadelphia.

The Flyers Cup championship was established in 1980 as a post-season tournament between the champions of the ICSHL, EHSHL, LBCSHL, and SHSHL to compete for the coveted Flyers Cup. The vision of the Flyers Cup was to send the winners to compete against the Western Pennsylvania champion for the overall state championship.

Archbishop Carroll, three-time champions of the ICSHL, won the first championship in 1980, defeating Malvern Prep of the EHSHL. Carroll followed up in 1981, winning the Flyers Cup for a second year, defeating Bishop Egan of the LBCSHL 9-0 at the Class of 1923 University of Pennsylvania Arena to earn a spot in the state championship. The Patriots defeated Western Pennsylvania champions North Catholic 4-3.

The Flyers Cup only crowned champions at the AAA level until 1991, when it began to hold tournaments at Class AA and A as well. In 1990, the state championships were given the title of Pennsylvania Cup, pitting the Penguins Cup champions against the Flyers Cup champions.

The birth of the Flyers Cup gave rise to the first high school hockey superstar in Archbishop Carroll's Scott "the Shot" Chamness, who scored 271 goals in 80 games over four years. In the 1980 Flyers Cup, he scored three hat tricks to lead the Patriots to the first Flyers Cup championship. Germantown Academy was led by goaltender Mike Richter, surrendering only 31 goals in 19 games in 1981-1982 and then holding off the Bishop Egan attack of Vince McNamee (59 goals) and Bob Lawrence (45 goals) in the 1983 Flyers Cup for a 9-5 victory.

Western Pennsylvania high school hockey was established in the spring of 1971 with six schools. Churchill and Penn Hills played the very first game, and Allderdice, Mt. Lebanon, Upper St. Clair, and West Mifflin also fielded teams. The Western Pennsylvania High School Hockey League began play in 1971-1972 at the Alpine Ice Chalet in Swissvale, Pennsylvania. In 1972-1973, the league, also known as the WPIHL, expanded to 19 teams for its second season.

For the 1973-1974 season, the Ohio Valley League, the South Penn High School Hockey League, and the Lake Shore Hockey League (LKSHL) were established in Northwestern Pennsylvania. The

South Hills Interscholastic Hockey League (SHIHL) was born in 1979-1980 at the Mt. Lebanon Ice Center and increased in 1987 as the South Penn High School Hockey League teams joined it.

In 1999, the LKSHL, SHIHL, and WPIHL merged to form the Pennsylvania Interscholastic Hockey League (PIHL). Teams are placed in Class A, AA, or AAA levels based on school size for the regular season and Penguins Cup playoffs.

Mt. Lebanon won the first league championship in 1972, defeating Penn Hills in overtime 5-4 to capture the first Western Pennsylvania high school hockey championship. In the 1972-1973 season, Pat McDermott of Mt. Lebanon was the first player in Western Pennsylvania to score 50 goals in a season. He finished the year with 55 goals, a record that stood until 1980. Churchill won nine WPIHL championships from 1973 to 1984.

Allderdice forward Buddy Martin set the new high-water mark for goals in a season with 65 in 1979-1980. He did so in one of the most competitive divisions ever seen in the area, and linemate Dee Rizzo contributed to the effort with 78 assists. The single-season record for goals lasted only one year before Lynn Sipe of North Catholic found the back of the net 68 times in 1980-1981. This new mark survived the 1980s until John Mooney of Serra Catholic scored over 100 goals in a single season, 1988, followed by Jon Johnson of Ford City in 1989 and Mike Sargo of Gateway High School in 1996.

The Penguins Cup was established in 1980. It included schools from the WPIHL, SHIHL, and LKSHL. The first championship was won by Upper St. Clair. The Penguins Cup was competed for at the Class AAA and AA levels until 1989, when the Class A level was added for both the Penguins Cup and state championships.

The Pennsylvania high school hockey championships were founded in 1975 in Erie, Pennsylvania. Baldwin defeated Churchill 4-3 in overtime to take home the first state AAA title. Richland, Erie McDowell, Springfield, and Bishop Neumann also participated in the inaugural state championships. Churchill established itself as the first dynasty in state history by winning its second state championship in 1979.

Today, the Pennsylvania Cup high school hockey championships are competed for by the winners of the Flyers Cup and the Penguins Cup, alternating between Eastern and Western Pennsylvania each year. In 45 years of the state championships, there have been dynasties, including Meadville High School with eight championships, West Chester Bayard Rustin with seven, and LaSalle College Prep School with six. Bethel Park, Bishop McCort, and Peters Township have each won five. LaSalle College Prep School has won ten Flyers Cups, and Meadville High School has won nine Penguins Cups to lead the way for Eastern and Western Pennsylvania, respectively.

One

THE 1970s
CHAMPIONSHIPS

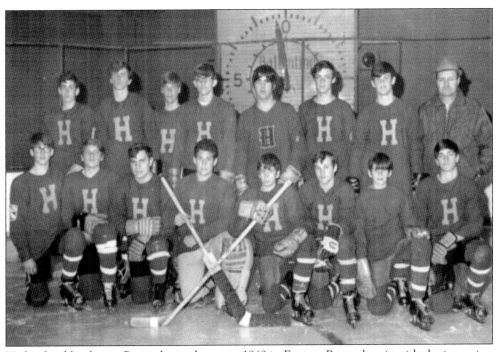

High school hockey in Pennsylvania began in 1969 in Eastern Pennsylvania with the inception of the Inter-County Scholastic Hockey League. Conestoga, O'Hara, Haverford, Swarthmore, Marple Newtown, Malvern Prep, and St. Joseph's were the first established programs. Conestoga won the ICSHL championship in the first three years. In 1971, Western Pennsylvania high school hockey was established with six schools when Churchill and Penn Hills played the first game and Allderdice, Mt. Lebanon, Upper St. Clair, and West Mifflin also fielded teams. The Western Pennsylvania High School Hockey League began play in 1971-1972 at the Alpine Ice Chalet in Swissvale. Churchill won nine WPIHL championships from 1973 to 1984. The Pennsylvania high school hockey championships were founded in 1975 in Erie. Baldwin defeated Churchill 4-3 in overtime to take home the first state AAA title. Richland, Erie McDowell, Springfield, and Bishop Neumann participated in the inaugural championships. The first three years featured a round-robin format of schools from Eastern and Western Pennsylvania at the Class AAA and AA levels (1976 and 1977). Churchill established itself as the first dynasty, winning its second state championship in 1979. (Courtesy of EPIHA.)

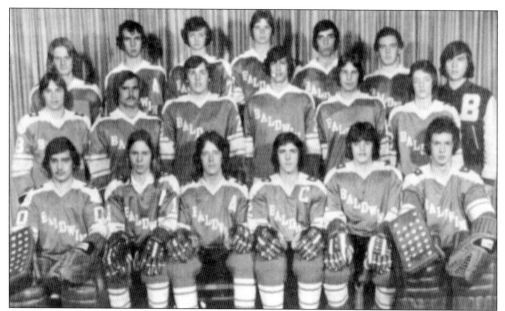

In 1975 in Erie, the Baldwin Highlanders defeated Erie McDowell 4-3 and Springfield of Philadelphia 2-1 in overtime to earn a spot in the first state championship. Baldwin faced WPIHL rival Churchill, and the teams battled to a 3-3 tie through regulation. Jim Cox's overtime goal at 1:10 of the extra session gave Baldwin the first state championship. Goaltender Brad Allman made 23 saves and was named along with Cox to the all-tournament team. Verne Shaver scored twice for Churchill. (Courtesy of the Pennsylvania Hockey Foundation Archives.)

In 1976, Mt. Lebanon enjoyed a 14-0-8 record in the regular season. In the state championships held in Pittsburgh, Mt. Lebanon defeated Haverford of Philadelphia 4-2 and Cardinal O'Hara of Philadelphia 3-1 to earn a spot in the 1976 state championship game at the Civic Arena. The Blue Devils gained redemption from their only loss of the season with a 4-2 victory over Churchill as Rob McArthur scored two goals and Mark DeGiovanni and Shane Galloway added goals for Mt. Lebanon, and goaltender Rich Cunningham was named MVP. (Courtesy of the Pennsylvania Hockey Foundation Archives.)

In the 1976 state final game at the Civic Arena, Abington scored first on a goal by Mark Leegard. Gateway rallied on goals by Tom Miller and Rick Fitchwell. The Ghosts rallied to take the lead 3-2 in the third period, setting up a heroic goal by John Liprando with 16 seconds remaining in regulation. Abington won this one in overtime as team captain Dennis Garvin scored on a power play with 51 seconds remaining to give the Ghosts the first state AA championship, handing Gateway its first loss under head coach Fran Czemerda. (Courtesy of the Pennsylvania Hockey Foundation Archives.)

In 1977, Churchill enjoyed a 22-0-0 record in the regular season under head coach Dan Sheehy. In the state championships held in Philadelphia, the Chargers defeated William Tennent, West Chester, and Richland to earn a spot in their third-straight championship. In the championship game, Churchill held off a rally from the Erie McDowell Trojans to win 6-5. Chuck Copeland scored a hat trick, along with goals from Brian Sheehy and Jack Foster, to lead the Chargers to their first state title. (Courtesy of the Pennsylvania Hockey Foundation Archives.)

Entering the 1977 championships, Fairview had a nucleus of juniors and sophomores led by James Cross, Matt Glass, Garett Regelman, and goaltender Scot Root. The Tigers swept through the preliminary round over South Park, rival Erie Cathedral Prep, and Penn Hills, 6-5, to gain a spot in the semifinals against North Catholic. The Tigers defeated the Trojans of North Catholic to gain a spot in the finals against Penn Hills, who defeated Moon 4-3. In the state championship, Fairview defeated Penn Hills. (Courtesy of Fairview High School.)

In 1979, Churchill enjoyed a 19-1-0 record in the regular season under head coach Dan Sheehy. The Chargers won their sixth WPIHL crown over Mt. Lebanon, 3-2. Churchill faced Erie McDowell in the final. In game one, Churchill defeated McDowell 8-4 as Frank Spena scored a hat trick, Toby Ritner added a pair of goals, and Kevin Monaco added four assists. In game two, McDowell defeated the Chargers 5-2 by scoring four second-period goals and making the total goals in the series 10-9 in favor of Churchill for its second-straight state title. (Courtesy of the Pennsylvania Hockey Foundation Archives.)

In 1979, South Hills Catholic defeated Central Catholic and State College to gain a spot in the state finals against North Catholic. In the championship, North Catholic jumped out to a 3-2 lead on goals by Chuck Chiatto, Mike Bagnato, and Larry Gaus, and South Hills Catholic countered with goals by B.J. Wetzel and Billy Siegfried. The Rebels took the lead on goals by Ray Jay Finch, Seigfried, and Gary Leckenby, 5-3. South Hills Catholic held on as the Trojans' Chuck Spatafore scored to cut the lead to 5-4, and the Rebels captured their first state championship. (Courtesy of Lenny Semplice.)

Two

THE 1980s CHAMPIONSHIPS

In 1981, the Pennsylvania high school hockey championships were given the title Pennsylvania Cup and adopted a format that pits the Penguins Cup champions of Western Pennsylvania against the Flyers Cup champions of Eastern Pennsylvania. Under the new name and format in 1981, Archbishop Carroll defeated North Catholic for the first Pennsylvania Cup crown, 4-3. In the Flyers Cup, Archbishop Carroll, three-time champions of the ICSHL, won the first title in 1980, defeating Malvern Prep. Carroll followed up in 1981, winning the Flyers Cup for a second consecutive year, defeating Bishop Egan of the LBCSHL 9-0. Germantown Academy won the Flyers Cup in 1982 and 1983 and the state championship in 1983, defeating Bethel Park 3-1. In Western Pennsylvania, the Penguins Cup was established in 1980 with schools from the LKSHL, SHIHL, and WPIHL. The Penguins Cup was competed for at the Class AAA and AA levels until 1989, when the Class A level was added. The list of championship teams completing perfect seasons during the 1980s included Conestoga in 1986, Upper St. Clair in 1987, and Meadville in 1989. (Courtesy of EPIHA.)

Archbishop Carroll had a 26-1-0 record entering the 1981 state final against undefeated North Catholic. In the championship game, Archbishop Carroll edged North Catholic 4-3 in a thriller at the University of Pennsylvania. North Catholic trailed the entire game and rallied from a two-goal deficit twice but was unable to gain the equalizer. Jeff Arnold scored twice, including the eventual game winner late in the second period. The Patriots outshot North Catholic 21-8. Frank Burdo and Phil Chamness scored for Carroll, and the Trojans' goals were scored by Lynn Sipe, Chuck Chiatto, and George Schuster. In the 1981 playoffs, Eastern Pennsylvania did not send any representatives for the Class AA division. Fairview defeated Seton LaSalle, and Hampton gained a spot against Thomas Jefferson. In the championship game, Fairview scored three first-period goals to gain a 3-0 lead. Thomas Jefferson battled back by scoring three times in the second period to tie the game 3-3 heading into the third period. Fairview scored the go-ahead goal with a little over two minutes to play in regulation on a power play to give the Tigers their second state championship. (Courtesy of EPIHA.)

Germantown Academy won the 1982 Flyers Cup 5-0 but was unable to field a team. In the 1982 AAA final, the game went back and forth as West Chester established a 5-2 lead. Baldwin rallied for three goals and tied the game at 6-6 with four minutes remaining. West Chester's Doug Bowman was the hero as he scored the game winner with 35 seconds remaining in the final period to give West Chester their first state championship. Baldwin's Ray Conway led the Highlanders with a pair of goals, and West Chester's Kyle Mundt and Tony Lassoy scored twice. (Courtesy of West Chester High School.)

In the 1982 state playoffs, Eastern Pennsylvania did not send any representatives for the Class AA division. Fairview defeated North Hills 8-1 and Canevin 6-5 to gain a spot in the championship against Central Catholic, winners over Chartiers Valley, 6-4, and Hampton, 1-0. In the championship game, Fairview scored an 8-3 victory over Central Catholic to give the Tigers their third state championship. (Courtesy of Fairview High School.)

The Germantown Academy Patriots (24-3-1) made the 1983 Flyers Cup finals and faced Bishop Egan (24-0-0) at the University City Center. Before 1,470 people, Germantown defeated Bishop Egan 9-5. In the final in Johnstown, Germantown's Mike McGregor scored in the second to give the Flyers Cup champs a 1-0 lead. Bethel's Joe Barbara tied the game at 1-1. Germantown's Ben Wurts scored the eventual game winner in the second period, and Mike McGregor added an empty netter as Germantown Academy goaltender Mike Richter shut the door and gave the Patriots their first championship 3-1 over Bethel Park. (Courtesy of EPIHA.)

Canevin defeated Greensburg Central Catholic 4-3 to advance to the west regional finals. Chartiers Valley advanced to the finals with a victory over North Hills 6-5 and Westmont Hilltop 4-3 to advance to the state finals at the Cambria County War Memorial. In the championship, Canevin defeated rival Chartiers Valley 4-2. The Crusaders were led by Greg Timmons with a hat trick, Tim Hegerty with three assists, and a great goaltending performance by Eric Antkiewicz, who stopped 37 of 39 shots. Canevin's head coach was Roger Oldaker. (Courtesy of the Pennsylvania Hockey Foundation Archives.)

In 1984, Cathedral Prep won the Lake Shore League and was awarded the No. 1 seed in the Penguins Cup playoffs. The Ramblers defeated Kittanning, Mt. Lebanon, and Baldwin to capture the title. In the 1984 Flyers Cup, Archbishop Ryan defeated Conestoga, Monsignor Bonner, Springfield, and Council Rock to capture its first Flyers Cup. In the state final, Cathedral Prep of Erie defeated Archbishop Ryan 4-1 on the strength of two goals from Chris Crane, goals by Tim Presta and Matt Guvula, and the goaltending of Tim Swail to capture their first crown for coach Nels White. (Courtesy of Pete McCormick.)

In 1984, Canevin assaulted the Penguins Cup field, outscoring opponents 25-4 in victories over Hampton, Ringgold, and Norwin in the western final. The Philadelphia representative was an SHSHL team that did not qualify for the Flyers Cup playoffs and had a sub-.500 record in league play. In the AA state title game, Canevin outlasted a pesky Archbishop Wood 7-5 to win its second consecutive state championship. The Crusaders were led by Greg Timmons, who scored the game-winning goal with a little over six minutes to play in the third period. (Courtesy of the Pennsylvania Hockey Foundation Archives.)

Conestoga advanced to the Flyers Cup in 1985 and was beaten by Cherry Hill East of the South Jersey Hockey League in the finals for their only loss of the 1984-1985 season. Conestoga became the Eastern Pennsylvania representative in the state championship against Mt. Lebanon at Face Off Circle in Warminster. The Pioneers took home their first state title, defeating the Blue Devils 6-4 on the strength of four goals from Scott Cowan and a penalty shot goal from Chip Graham for Conestoga head coach John Titus, whose team finished 24-1-0. (Courtesy of Mike Graves.)

Canevin earned its third consecutive Western Pennsylvania AA title with wins over Meadville in overtime, State College, and Chartiers Valley in the western regional final. In the AA final in Warminster, Pennsbury broke out in the second period to a 3-0 lead on goals by Joe Enders, Dave Fisher, and Scott Junk. Mike Hegarty got the Crusaders on the board to make the score 3-1 early in the third period. Goaltender Scott Teeter made 28 saves as Pennsbury outshot Canevin 32-29 to give the Falcons their first state title. (Courtesy of Conestoga Hockey.)

Conestoga enjoyed a perfect 26-0-0 record in the regular season in the ICSHL. In the Flyers Cup playoffs, the Pioneers defeated Pennsbury in the semifinals and advanced to the finals. In the two-game championship series against Malvern Prep, Conestoga defeated the Friars to capture the school's first Eastern Pennsylvania championship. In the state championship, Conestoga defeated Penguins Cup champions Upper St. Clair 4-2 to cap a 30-0-0 perfect season. (Courtesy of Taylor Railton.)

In 1986, Chartiers Valley knocked off Ford City and State College to earn a spot in the finals against Meadville. Before a packed house at Mt. Lebanon Rec Center, the Colts prevailed 6-4 to win the Western Pennsylvania championship. Chartiers Valley earned a spot in the state championship against Archbishop Wood out of the Suburban League, which finished third in the Flyers Cup tournament. In the state final, Chartiers Valley dominated Archbishop Wood as Tim Tracy scored four times to give the Colts and coach Eddie Schultz their first state championship. (Courtesy of Ed Schultz.)

Upper St. Clair marched through the 1987 season undefeated at 22-0-0. The Panthers were led by brothers Pete and Phil Shaffalo, Dave Klasnick, Eric Baumgartner, and Dean Wegner and the goaltending of Jim McVay. They swept through the playoffs, defeating Westmont Hilltop, Erie Cathedral Prep, and rivals Mt. Lebanon in the Penguins Cup 10-2. In the Pennsylvania final, the Panthers defeated Flyers Cup champions Malvern Prep on an overtime goal by Chris Wittemore. The win capped a perfect season for Upper St. Clair to match the 1986 AAA champs Conestoga. (Courtesy of Dave Klasnick.)

The Meadville hockey program under Jamie Plunkett played the 1987 season in the LKSHL and had a 19-3-2 overall record. The Bulldogs advanced to the state finals with victories over Steel Valley, Beaver, and State College, 4-2. In the state championship at the Face Off Circle in Warminster, Meadville defeated Council Rock 5-3. The state title was the first in Meadville's storied history under coach Plunkett. (Courtesy of Meadville Bulldog Hockey.)

In the 1988 playoffs, Baldwin defeated Westmont Hilltop, Upper St. Clair, and Shadyside Academy on the strength of a hat trick from Bob Reed. In the 1988 finals, Archbishop Wood took a 1-0 lead as Jim Conlon scored. Baldwin tied the score in the second period as Joe Labellarte scored on a power play. The Highlanders took the lead for good in the third period as Bob Reed scored to make it 2-1. Joe Labellarte and Bob Reed added insurance goals as Baldwin outshot Archbishop Wood 46-17, and goaltender Jason Byers earned the championship win. (Courtesy of Baldwin High School.)

William Tennent opened up a 2-0 lead as Ryan Maestas scored twice. The Dragons' James Thompson cut the lead to 2-1. Maestas completed the hat trick just 23 seconds after Allderdice scored and set up Mike Mothersbaugh to give Tennent a 4-1 lead after the second. In the third, Maestas scored his fourth goal of the game on a breakaway to make it 5-1. Allderdice rallied as Barry Livestone and Dickie Rizzo scored to make the final 5-3 and give William Tennent their first state title. Panthers goaltender Scott Shaw turned aside 41 of 44 shots. (Courtesy of Jeff Garber.)

Meadville played the 1989 season with a 31-3-2 overall record and a 12-0-0 league record. They won the Penguins Cup with victories over Mt. Lebanon, Bethel Park, and Upper St. Clair. Goaltenders Jim McCarney and Mark Chandley surrendered only one goal in three games of the playoffs. In the state championship, Meadville defeated William Tennent 4-0. The game featured a shutout for goaltender Jim McCarney, a hat trick by Clayton Phillis, and a goal by Jason Wentland. The state title was the second under head coach Jamie Plunkett. (Courtesy of Meadville Bulldog Hockey.)

In the 1989 Penguins Cup, the Crusaders defeated Latrobe 5-2 and State College 5-2 to earn a spot opposite Bishop McCort, winners over Chartiers Valley 4-3 in double overtime and 1988 Penguins Cup champs Allderdice 5-2. In the Penguins Cup final, Canevin turned back Bishop McCort 4-3 in overtime. In the state final, Canevin capped off a remarkable comeback season, finishing second in the SHIHL AA standings and their fourth Penguins Cup championship and third state championship with a 2-1 victory over West Chester East. Co-coaches Bob Cupelli and Greg Timmons led the Crusaders to the state title. (Courtesy of Canevin High School.)

In 1989, Plum had a 20-1-1 record during the regular season, led by Joe Grande with 99 points and Anthony Asturi with 84. The Mustangs captured the Penguins Cup with wins over South Park, Hampton, and Greensburg Salem, 5-3. In the 1989 eastern playoffs, Cardinal O'Hara represented in the state finals despite not playing in the Flyers Cup. In the final, Plum completed a magical run through the western playoffs for their first Penguins Cup and first state championship with a 10-4 victory over Cardinal O'Hara. Coach Jim Murray led the Mustangs to the state title. (Courtesy of Mike McIntyre.)

Three

THE 1990S
CHAMPIONSHIPS

In 1991, the Pennsylvania high school hockey championships became more formal as the Flyers Cup added Class AA and A. This helped to have the Flyers Cup champions meet the Penguins Cup champions for the state title, alternating between Eastern and Western Pennsylvania each year. Western Pennsylvania's Meadville High School dominated the early state championships, winning six Penguins Cups and five Pennsylvania titles under head coach Jamie Plunkett. Eastern Pennsylvania's Bishop Conwell Egan completed the Pennsylvania hat trick, winning the Class A crown in 1990, Class AA crown in 1995, and Class AAA crown in 1999 under Rich Slack. The 1990s saw Bishop McCort dominate the Class A level, winning five times. Greensburg Central Catholic won the Class A title and Class AA title twice, and Thomas Jefferson closed out the 1990s with three championships. The list of championship teams completing perfect seasons began to grow during the 1990s as Meadville's regular seasons in the LKSHL and playoffs in 1993, 1994, 1995, and 1996 were perfect. Bishop McCort (in 1996) and Thomas Jefferson (in 1999) joined Meadville. (Courtesy of Don Powell.)

Malvern Prep won the Flyers Cup in 1990 with an 11-2 victory over William Tennent. In the 1990 Penguins Cup, Upper St. Clair defeated Meadville in the final, 4-0. Upper St. Clair opened the scoring as Dave Klasnick scored to make it 1-0. Malvern tied the game on a breakaway by Ben Coa and extended the lead to 4-1 on a hat trick by Keith Grimley. The Panthers' Darren Wegner scored a pair of goals to make it 4-3. Keith Haig and Grimley added goals to make it a 6-3 final and the first title for coach Bob Martin. (Courtesy of Malvern Prep High School.)

Father Judge gained a berth in the state final by defeating West Chester East. Johnstown had a 17-1-1 season and defeated Chartiers Valley 8-4 to capture the Penguins Cup. In the final, Father Judge raced to a 5-1 lead after two periods. Johnstown rallied behind a pair of goals each by Brian Bunn and Brian Wincer, to tie the game with 1:17 remaining. Father Judge got the game-winner with just four seconds on the clock as Mike Bill scored on a rebound to give coach Bill Conners his first state championship with a 6-5 victory. (Courtesy of Tom McGinley.)

Bishop Egan was LBCSHL runners-up under head coach Rich Slack in 1990. Ringgold took the 1990 Penguins Cup with wins over North Hills and Fox Chapel 3-2; it was the first time they won the title. In the state final, Bishop Egan employed a dump-and-chase strategy and cruised to a 5-1 victory to capture its first title. Joe Vecchione led the Eagles with two goals and an assist to an early 4-0 lead and never looked back. (Courtesy of Bishop Egan High School.)

In 1991, Council Rock defeated Malvern Prep in consecutive 3-2 games to win the Flyers Cup. Armstrong defeated Meadville 7-4 to capture its first title. In the final, Armstrong earned a 3-2 lead with a pair of goals from Aaron Faust and Jon Yackmack. Council Rock's Roman Bussetti scored his third goal of the game to tie it. Armstrong regained the lead 4-3 on a goal from Jason Jack. Council Rock rallied as Matt Hunter scored to tie the game. Council Rock's Chad Markowitz scored the game-winner to give the Indians their first championship, 5-4. (Courtesy of Tom McGinley.)

Beaver had a 17-2-0 record and defeated Plum 8-6 to advance to the championship. Undefeated Germantown Academy beat Haverford 5-4 to win its third Flyers Cup. In the final, Germantown made it a 2-0 lead on goals by Ryan Goldman and Damien Borichevsky. Beaver's Gary Taylor and Brad Frattarolli scored to tie the game in the second period. In the third, it was Brad Frattarolli again scoring 17 seconds into the third period to give the Bobcats the lead, 3-2. Beaver's Brian Frattarolli iced the game with 1:32 to play, giving Beaver its first title under coach Larry Gaus. (Courtesy of Jimmy Black.)

The 1991 season had teams compete at the AAA, AA, and A levels for the Flyers Cup. Monsignor Bonner defeated Archbishop Carroll and Archbishop Ryan 13-2 to earn the championship. State College made the most of its second Penguins Cup finals appearance, defeating Steel Valley 7-1. In the state final, Monsignor Bonner defeated State College 5-2. The win marked the first state crown for Monsignor Bonner for coach Ted Dolan's squad. (Courtesy of the Pennsylvania Hockey Foundation Archives.)

The year 1992 saw the Bulldogs beat 1991 champions Armstrong 8-5 for their third Penguins Cup. Monsignor Bonner captured its second-straight Flyers Cup, beating William Tennent 3-1 and 6-1. In the final, Monsignor Bonner scored the opening goal, but back came the Bulldogs as Scott Phillis, Mike McCarney, and Brandon Corey scored in less than two minutes to make it 3-1. The second period was all Meadville as Mike McCarney, Tom Westfall, and Dave Jones scored. The Bulldogs scored three more in the third as McCarney, Westfall, and Brett Messina scored to make it a 9-3 final. (Courtesy of Meadville Bulldog Hockey.)

Council Rock edged Malvern Prep again in the best of three Flyers Cup 2-1 to earn its second Flyers Cup title. Johnstown beat Franklin Regional as Brian Wincer scored the game winner to give Johnstown the Penguins Cup. In the final, Council Rock scored twice as Brian Green and Eric Kratchwell tallied to give the Indians a 2-0 lead. Council Rock extended the lead as Jaret Lyons and Kevin Dietch scored to make it 4-0. Goaltender Scott Prosek made 29 saves to earn a championship shutout and give coach Paul Gilligan and Council Rock their second consecutive state title. (Courtesy of Tom McGinley.)

The 1992 season saw the Haverford Fords earn their first Flyers Cup, defeating Pennsbury 6-3 and 7-2. Greensburg Central Catholic defeated Belle Vernon with a 6-1 victory to earn its first championship. In the final, the game was knotted 2-2 as the Fords' John Chalfont and Dave Gallagher scored and Greensburg got goals from Matt Kundrod and Chris Shoub. Haverford seized the lead with four unanswered goals from John Dwyer, Lou Ventura, Dave Gallagher, and Jim Northrup to take a 5-2 lead. Haverford scored two more times in the third for an 8-4 victory for coach Andy Rolli. (Courtesy of Christopher Cifone.)

The 1993 Meadville team was dominant, led by three 50-goal scorers in Ryan Smart, Tommy Westfall, and Scott Phillis. The Bulldogs beat North Allegheny, Shaler, and Bethel Park 7-1 to capture the Penguins Cup. In the Flyers Cup, Monsignor Bonner defeated Germantown 5-1 and 3-2. The final, played before a crowd of 2,000 in Haverford, saw Monsignor Bonner battle through a 1-1 game until Tommy Westfall scored to make it 2-1. Scott Phillis, Marc Johnson, and Jason Guerrierri added goals to give coach Jamie Plunkett his fourth championship in six years with a 5-1 victory. (Courtesy of Meadville Bulldog Hockey.)

In 1993, Father Judge defeated Cardinal O'Hara 3-2 and 7-1 to win its first Flyers Cup. Canevin won the Penguins Cup with a 6-3 victory over Franklin Regional as Paul Sikorksi recorded a hat trick. In the final, Canevin won 4-2 on goals by Jeremy Swegman, Greg Watkins, Paul Sikorski, and Jim Palmer. Judge's Greg Watkins and Matt Burlando accounted for the Judge goals. Father Judge rallied as John Palentine scored twice to tie the game and win the title as Eric Tysarczyk scored late in the final period to give coach Bill Conners his second title. (Courtesy of Tom McGinley.)

In the 1993 Penguins Cup, Greensburg Central Catholic defeated Bishop McCort 4-2 led by Jeff Adams. In the Flyers Cup, Pennsbury defeated Unionville. In the final, Greensburg raced to a 3-0 lead on a pair of goals by Jeff Adams and one by Chris O'Toole. Adams completed a four-goal game in the third period as the Centaurians captured their first crown 6-2. Jeremiah Allison added an insurance goal as Greensburg outshot Pennsbury 44-22 and goaltender Ben Turin earned the victory between the pipes for coach Butch Marrietta. (Courtesy of Jeff Adams.)

The 1994 Meadville team captured its third straight Penguins Cup beating North Allegheny, Mt. Lebanon, and Bethel Park 6-2. Meadville's Jason Guerrerri had a pair of goals, and Ryan Smart had three assists. In the 1994 Flyers Cup, Germantown Academy defeated Haverford. In the final, Patriots goaltender Sam Weiner was brilliant through two periods in a scoreless game. Meadville wore down Germantown, and Mike Teasdale gave the Bulldogs a 1-0 lead. Scott Phillis and Jason Guerrerri made it 3-0 as the Bulldogs captured their third straight title for coach Jamie Plunkett before 1,000 Meadville fans. (Courtesy of Meadville Bulldog Hockey.)

Greensburg Central Catholic defeated Franklin Regional 4-1 as Jeff Adams and Chris Shoub scored twice to give the Centaurians their third straight Penguins Cup in 1994. Conwell Egan won the Flyers Cup 4-3 over Upper Darby. In the final, Greensburg dominated Conwell Egan as Jeff Adams scored four times to lead the Centaurians to their second straight title. The Centaurians defense played a superb game, limiting the Conwell Egan offense. After the Eagles scored early in the third period, Jeff Adams scored his fourth, and Phil Rock and Chris Shoub added tallies for a 6-1 final for coach Butch Marrietta. (Courtesy of Jeff Adams.)

Bishop McCort finished the 1993–1994 season with a 14-4-3 record and won the Penguins Cup, defeating Seton LaSalle 8-1 as Greg Kutchma and Geoff Shiley scored two goals. Radnor lost to Washington Township of New Jersey in the Flyers Cup final but qualified as the state final representative. The final was no contest from the outset, as Bishop McCort scored five times in the opening period en route to a 9-1 victory to its first state championship. Brett Houston led the Crushers with a goal and four assists, and Kris Carlson scored three times for head coach Galen Head. (Courtesy of Bishop McCort Hockey.)

The Bulldogs captured their fourth straight Penguins Cup beating Penn Hills, North Allegheny, and Bethel Park 13-0. Meadville was led by hat tricks by Ron Pusz, Jason Guerrerri, and Toby Lang. Germantown Academy beat Downingtown in the Flyers Cup final 4-2 and 3-2 to capture its second straight crown. In the state final, Jason Guerrerri scored twice, and Jim Brunner made 18 saves to lead the Bulldogs to their fourth-consecutive title over Germantown Academy at Haverford Skatium, 4-1. Patriot star Radim Zelenka was stopped several times in the championship game by Brunner. (Courtesy of Meadville Bulldog Hockey.)

Conwell Egan defeated Malvern Prep 9-1 to capture consecutive Flyers Cups under coach Rich Slack. The 1995 Penguins Cup final was led by a pair of goals from Jim Abbott and Thad Fritz to win their second Penguins Cup with a 4-3 win over Franklin Regional. In the final, Conwell Egan built a lead in the opening period and never looked back, defeating North Catholic 7-4. The Eagles' Jason Suppin scored a hat trick, pacing a 3-1 lead after the first period and a 5-3 lead after two periods. Conwell Egan goaltender Brian Urban made 27 saves. (Courtesy of Alvina Tetley.)

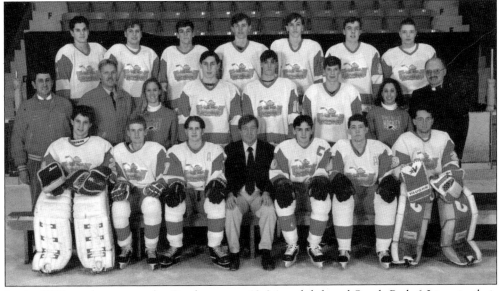

In the 1995 regular season, the Crushers went 18-0-1 and defeated South Park 6-2 to win their second-straight Penguins Cup title. The Crushers scored three shorthanded goals with two goals each from Greg Kutchma and Brett Houston. In the 1995 Flyers Cup, Unionville defeated Neshaminy 6-0 to capture its first Flyers Cup. In the final, Bishop McCort's prolific offense proved to be too much for Unionville, as the team cruised to a second consecutive state championship with a 9-1 victory at Haverford Skatium. Greg Kutchma, Kris Carlson, and Brett Houston scored two goals each for the Crimson Crushers. (Courtesy of Bishop McCort Hockey.)

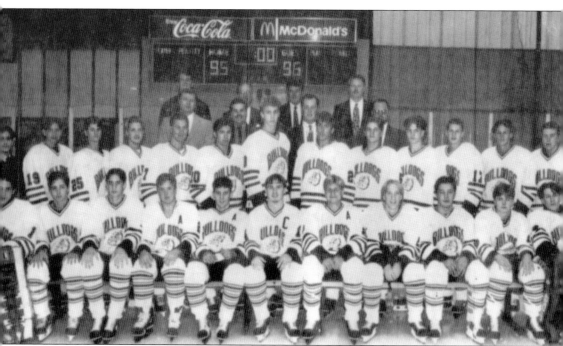

The Bulldogs captured their fifth straight Penguins Cup in 1996. Dan Leech scored the game winner in overtime with a 3-2 win over Upper St. Clair. The LaSalle Explorers shredded Germantown Academy 12-2 to win the Flyers Cup. In the final, the Bulldogs and Explorers battled to a 2-2 tie through regulation as Mike Chornack and Paul Rusilko scored for Meadville and Casey Schaffer and Brian Curci scored for LaSalle. Meadville overcame LaSalle at 12:35 of overtime as Mike Chornack buried a slapshot past goaltender Patrick McCullion to win the team's fifth straight title, 3-2, for Jamie Plunkett, outshooting LaSalle 40-8. (Courtesy of Meadville Bulldog Hockey.)

In the 1996 Penguins Cup, Indiana raced to a 3-1 lead on the strength of a hat trick by Steve Putt. Greensburg Central Catholic rallied behind two goals from Phil Rock, and Ryan Davis scored in overtime to defeat Indiana. In the championship, Greensburg faced Flyers Cup champions Upper Darby. The Centaurians opened up a 4-0 lead on goals by Jordan Spallone, Phil Rock, Derek Galbraith, and Ben Komolos. Upper Darby rallied to close the gap to 4-3. Jordan Spallone sealed the victory for Greensburg, and goaltender Jon Vesely made 26 saves to earn the title. (Courtesy of Butch and Helen Marrietta.)

Bishop McCort breezed to a 19-0-0 record and the Penguins Cup win over West Allegheny. St. Pius X beat Bensalem to capture its first Flyers Cup. In the final, the War Memorial crowd of 3,732 was the largest ever to attend a state final. Greg Kutchma and Josh Piro scored two goals each, and St. Pius X's Mark Sharbak completed the hat trick in a 5-5 game. Josh Piro and Greg Kutchma scored in the third to give Bishop McCort a 7-5 lead, and goaltender John Brezovec shutout the rest of the way for St. Pius X to give the Crushers their third-straight state championship under head coach Galen Head. (Courtesy of Bishop McCort Hockey.)

In the 1997 Penguins Cup finals at the Civic Arena, Bethel Park defenseman Keith Stanich fired a laser with 48 seconds remaining to give the Blackhawks their second Penguins Cup win, 3-2. In the 1997 Flyers Cup final, Malvern Prep beat Council Rock in the best-of-three series. In the state final at Ice Line, Bethel Park built a lead and held off a Malvern Prep 4-3 rally to capture its first state championship. Michael Gastgeb and Jim Lilja scored two goals each, and goaltender Nick Lordi made 17 saves to earn the victory. (Courtesy of Nick Santora.)

Cathedral Prep defeated Fox Chapel 8-2 in the Penguins Cup final to earn its first title in 13 years. Prep's John Major and Jon Will scored two goals each. The Conestoga Pioneers beat Bensalem 8-3 to earn a spot in the state finals at Ice Line. In the final, Mike Graves gave Conestoga a 1-0 lead. Cathedral Prep exploded for four unanswered goals by Jourdan Legace, Aaron Cross, Casey Dougherty, and Jake Predis, and John Major and Greg Rogers added goals in the second period as the Ramblers coasted 6-1 to capture their second state championship for head coach Nels White. (Courtesy of Cathedral Prep Hockey.)

In 1997, the Crimson Crushers bested Pine Richland in the Penguins Cup final, 2-1, led by goals from Kris Carlson and Josh Piro. Cheltenham beat Marple Newtown 7-2 to capture its first Flyers Cup. The Crushers had a combined shutout for goaltenders Nick Mish and John Brezovec, who faced only 14 shots in the victory. The state final was the Kris Carlson and Josh Piro show as the four-time Pennsylvania champions blanked Cheltenham 7-0 at the Ice Line in West Chester. (Courtesy of Bishop McCort Hockey.)

In 1998, the LaSalle Explorers won their second Flyers Cup in three years, edging Germantown Academy 4-3. In the Penguins Cup, Central Catholic beat Meadville with two goals each from Teague Willetts-Kelly and Bernie Chmiel. In the final, Central and LaSalle battled to a 2-2 tie into the third. Billy Downey and Joe Grzandziel scored for the Vikings, and Sean Heron and Drew Santillo scored for the Explorers. LaSalle won the face-off late in the third, and Peter Naticchione scored on a wrist shot, beating Kris Mayotte and giving the Explorers a 3-2 championship win for coach Wally Muehlbronner. (Courtesy of Wally Muehlbronner.)

In 1998, Don Powell and Thomas Jefferson faced a strong Class AA field, edging 1997 finalists Fox Chapel 7-6 and two-time state champions Greensburg Central Catholic 8-5 to advance to the Penguins Cup for the first time since 1981. In the final at Rostraver Ice Garden, Thomas Jefferson spotted Peters Township a 1-0 lead and rallied on goals by Brian Hartman, Pat Kenny, and Chuck Fink to win its first Penguins Cup 3-1. Unionville beat Palmyra 10-5 and Ridley 7-1 and then defeated Archbishop Ryan 5-4 to win their second Flyers Cup. In the state final, Thomas Jefferson struck first on the power play as Chuck Fink scored at 7:18. Michael Roth extended the Jaguars' lead to 2-0 with another goal with 3:22 to go in the opening period. Unionville rallied in the second period, finally breaking through on Matt Mitchell as Charlie Gerbron scored at 5:16 to cut the lead to 2-1. This state championship took a different turn in the third period as Thomas Jefferson scored five times. Chuck Fink scored twice to complete the hat trick and Pat Kenny added a pair of goals as the Jaguars outshot Unionville 13-6 and held off the Indians, who scored four times for a final score of 7-5 in favor of Thomas Jefferson, which won its first state AA championship. (Courtesy of Don Powell.)

In 1997-1998, Seton LaSalle defeated Shadyside Academy 3-1 and West Allegheny 6-2 to reach its first Penguins Cup finals. The Rebels battled Westmont Hilltop to a 2-2 tie into the second period on goals from J.B. Bittner and John Plack, and Louie Garritan scored the game winner with a pass from Brandon LaBoon to beat Hiltoppers goaltender Adam Curry with 8:29 remaining. The Garnet Valley Jaguars won the Flyers Cup by defeating Dallastown 8-1, Radnor 2-1, and Pennsbury in the final 4-2 at the Spectrum to win their first championship in school history. In the state final at Rostraver Ice Garden, Seton LaSalle jumped to an early 2-0 lead on goals by Landon Fries and Christopher Panucci. Garnet Valley fought back to tie the game on power play goals by Mike Pacitti and Steve Knech. The Rebels went back in the lead on a goal by Mark Morton in the second period and extended the lead 14 seconds into the third on a goal by Louie Garritan to make it 4-2. The Jaguars rallied again to tie the game with goals by Tony Cole and Mike Pacitti five minutes in. Seton LaSalle would not be denied, as Brandon LaBoon blasted a slap shot home with 6:48 remaining to give the Rebels the lead again. When Louie Garritan added an empty netter in the game's final minute, Seton LaSalle claimed its second state title in school history for coach Jeff Brooks. The Rebels were led by LaBoon and Garritan, who both tallied over 50 goals for the season. (Courtesy of Kurt Ross.)

In the 1999 Flyers Cup final, Conwell Egan was outshot 51-19 but overcame Malvern 6-5 on a goal by Michael Delfin in overtime. In the Penguins Cup, the Bulldogs outlasted Central Catholic as Nick Tucci scored in overtime. In the final, Meadville played Conwell Egan before a packed house at the Grundy. Egan's Nick Caruso and Mitch LaFleur scored, and Nick Tucci and Ryan Minik scored for Meadville. At 2:10 of the third overtime, Brian Tetley fired home a wrist shot to give the Eagles their third state title with a 3-2 win over the Bulldogs for coach Rich Slack. (Courtesy of the EPHIA.)

Undefeated Thomas Jefferson defeated Cathedral Prep, led by a hat trick from John Zeiler and four points for Brian Hartman in a 7-0 win. LaSalle beat Holy Ghost Prep 3-0 to win the 1999 Flyers Cup. In the final, Thomas Jefferson was looking for history and dominated LaSalle from the outset, outshooting the Explorers 44-14. Chuck Fink scored a hat trick, D.J. Morgele added two goals, and Matt Mitchell and Joe Essey combined for a shutout for a 7-0 state championship victory and a perfect season for coach Don Powell. (Courtesy of Thomas Jefferson Hockey.)

The Crushers won their fifth Penguins Cup against Richland Cambria 8-0, led by eight different goal scorers and a shutout for goaltender Chris Cuppett. Archbishop Ryan won the 1999 Flyers Cup, defeating Springfield 6-4. In the final, Bishop McCort scored five times in the opening period to build a 5-2 lead by a pair of goals from Garrett Oakes. McCort outskated Archbishop Ryan and outshot them 40-19 en route to a 9-3 championship win. Oakes completed the hat trick, Todd Kamzik added a pair of goals, and Tim George netted three points for the Crimson Crushers. (Courtesy of Bishop McCort Hockey.)

Four

THE 2000S
CHAMPIONSHIPS

The state championships grew in numbers in the 2000s, as Western Pennsylvania merged its leagues into the PIHL in 1999. The Penguins Cup playoffs had a qualification process during the regular season that seeded the schools. Eastern Pennsylvania also grew in numbers, as over 100 schools participated and were eligible for the Flyers Cup playoffs. The ICSHL, LBCSHL, EHSHL, and SHSHL welcomed the Central Pennsylvania Interscholastic Hockey League and Lehigh Valley Interscholastic Hockey League to the Flyers Cup championships. The 2000s saw several runs of championships as Bethel Park dominated the Class AAA level, winning four times to go with their first title in 1997. Serra Catholic won three Class A championships, Peters Township won three Class AA crowns, and Latrobe closed out the decade with three titles. The list of championship teams completing perfect seasons began to grow during the 2000s, with Bethel Park AAA in 2002, Mt. Lebanon AAA in 2006, and Latrobe AA in 2009. (Courtesy of PIHL.)

During the 2000 season, Bethel Park went 21-1-1 and captured the Penguins Cup over Cathedral Prep. Bethel freshman Grady Clingan scored twice, and the team edged Cathedral Prep 5-4. Jay Giftos scored a hat trick for the Ramblers. The Hawks won their first state title since 1997 in 2000, beating Father Judge 3-1 at the Civic Arena. Justin Glock scored twice, and Matthew Shack added another for Bethel Park, as they outshot the Crusaders 37-21. Brian Bakowski made 20 saves in goal to give coach Jim McVay and Bethel Park their second state championship in school history. (Courtesy of Bethel Park Hockey.)

Thomas Jefferson finished 24-1-0 during the 2000 regular season and beat Canevin in the Penguins Cup 2-1 on a Brian Hartman goal with 23 seconds remaining in regulation. In the state final, Thomas Jefferson opened up a 3-1 lead in the opening period, and the Jaguars added three more in the third to cruise to a 6-1 victory over Archbishop Carroll. Goaltender Joe Essey continued with terrific play, stopping 37 of 38 shots. Goals came from John Zeiler with a pair, along with D.J. Morgele, Patrick Kenney, Don Holtz, and E.J. Greco to give Thomas Jefferson its third straight championship. (Courtesy of PIHL.)

The 2000 Serra Catholic team went 17-1-0, and in the Penguins Cup final, goaltender Jordan Synkowski stole the show with 29 saves in a 4-1 victory as Brandon Plosinka, Gary Klapkowski, Riley McKelvey, and Chris Darcy scored for the Eagles. Pennsbury earned its second Flyers Cup championship with a 3-2 victory over Strath Haven. In the final, Serra Catholic skated to a 3-0 lead on goals by Gordan Eland, Gary Klapkowski, and P.J. Mastylak. Mastylak scored his second goal and held off Pennsbury until the team broke Jordan Synkowski's shutout bid to give Serra Catholic its first state championship. (Courtesy of Chris Darcy.)

Bethel Park enjoyed a 22-1-0 regular season, yielding only 23 goals in 23 games behind the goaltending of Andrew Torcchia and its stellar defense led by Dan Mackin and Tom Starkey. In the Penguins Cup at the Cambria County War Memorial, the Hawks shut down Allderdice 7-3 to capture their second consecutive Penguins Cup title, led by Justin Glock, Dan Kornosky, and Lee Volensky. In the state final, Bethel Park shut down the high-scoring attack from Flyers Cup champions Malvern Prep 2-1 at the Haverford Skatium. (Courtesy of Bethel Park Hockey.)

Beaver had a 17-3-1 record in 2001 and won the Penguins Cup, defeating Pine Richland 4-1 at the Cambria War Memorial. Beaver moved on to the state final against Flyers Cup champs Archbishop Carroll at the Haverford Skatium. The Bobcats' offensive display of 35 goals in five games and 14 against continued into the state finals, as Beaver defeated the Patriots of Archbishop Carroll 8-4, led by the top line of Danny and Doug Miller and Dustin Hawthorne for head coach Bob Hawthorne. (Courtesy of Beaver Hockey.)

Springfield won the Flyers Cup, defeating Conwell Egan in the finals. The 2001 Serra Eagles won the Penguins Cup 6-3 over Bishop McCort at the War Memorial. Springfield played a terrific opening period and a half to gain a 3-0 lead. Serra's Chris Darcy completed the hat trick midway through the third period to tie the game at 3-3. Freshman goaltender Timmy Johnson was stellar, stopping 34 Cougars shots. Serra freshman B.J. Depaoli scored the game winner with 33 seconds left, and Jesse Lubasch added an empty netter to make it 5-3, giving coach John Mooney his second straight title. (Courtesy of PIHL.)

50

Bethel Park and Malvern Prep ran through the Penguins Cup and Flyers Cup in 2002. In the final, Bethel Park's Dan Zabkar scored in the opening period to give Bethel a 1-0 lead. Brett Watson scored for Malvern to tie the game. Michael Curran found the rebound and backhanded it home to give the Friars a 2-1 lead 1:58 away from the state championship. Tony Sands beat Sorenstrom with 1:34 remaining and sent it to overtime. In overtime, C.J. Strauss's long shot hit Justin Glock and found its way behind Sorenstrom, and Bethel Park won its third straight state championship. (Courtesy of Bethel Park Blackhawks.)

Peters Township went 18-1-0 during the regular season and captured its first Penguins Cup with a 4-2 win over Indiana. In the final against Archbishop Carroll, Peters built a 3-1 lead on goals by Matt Schwartz, Christian Hanson, and Mike Papciak in the second. Stefano Teece scored early for Carroll to cut the lead to 3-2, but Hanson and Matt Schwartz extended the lead to 5-2. Hanson, Papciak, Chris Clackson, and Jeremy Simmons added goals in the final 7:30 to make the outcome a convincing 10-3 victory over Archbishop Carroll. (Courtesy of PIHL.)

The 2002 state final was a tightly fought contest and went wire to wire. The teams battled through two periods tied at 4-4 as Dustin Songer, Steve Leppo, C.J King, and Joey Manning scored for Serra, and Eddie Devine (with a pair of goals), Chris Brennan, and John Brennan scored for Radnor. With 3:10 remaining in the third period, a Radnor defenseman clearing-up attempt found Serra's Devon Kane, who made no mistake, beating Danner and giving Serra a 5-4 lead. The Serra Eagles held off Radnor for a 5-4 heart-stopping third straight championship for coach John Mooney. (Courtesy of Chris Darcy.)

Malvern Prep had to feel a sigh of relief after they defeated the LaSalle team 2-1 to win the Flyers Cup. Meadville defeated Franklin Regional in the Penguins Cup, 8-3. In the final, Malvern Prep's Mike Curran and Chris Campanale scored before Meadville's D.J. Durkee made it 2-1. In the second, the teams traded goals as Campanale and Justin Martin scored for the Friars and Christian Nickerson and Justin Wehrle tallied for the Bulldogs. Meadville's Chris Claspy tied the game at 4-4, and Christian Nickerson poked home a rebound to give Meadville a 5-4 victory and Penguins Cup number eight in dramatic fashion. (Courtesy of Meadville Bulldogs Hockey.)

In 2003, Holy Ghost Prep (19-1-4) defeated West Chester Henderson in overtime to capture the Flyers Cup. Peters Township defeated Kittanning 6-3 to capture the Penguins Cup. In the final, Peters Township came out flying with goals by Matt Clackson, Mike Papciak, Matt Schwartz, and Brandon Rubeo. The teams traded goals in the second period as Matt Schwartz and Mike Sherer scored and Ryan Gunderson and Paul Worthington scored to cut the lead to 6-2. Christian Minella, with a pair of goals, and Kevin Kustron brought home a 9-3 second straight championship. (Courtesy of Bill Hammonds.)

Westmont Hilltop upended Serra Catholic 4-3 in the Penguins Cup. In the Flyers Cup, Radnor demolished the competition in four games, 31-4, to put themselves in the state championship. Chris Brennan finished off with a great move on the forehand, putting the Raiders on top 1-0. The Hilltoppers' Brian Willet blasted a slap shot past Ek to tie the game at 1-1. The Raiders scored on the power play as Brennan and Nick Ryder found Ed Devine, who buried a wrist shot to give Radnor the lead 2-1 with 6:58 remaining. Radnor held on for the win. (Courtesy of EPIHA.)

Malvern Prep defeated Holy Ghost Prep in the Flyers Cup 6-4. In the final, Malvern's Justin Martin opened the scoring before Mt. Lebanon's Dan Wilen and Bryan Colligan gave Mt. Lebanon a 2-1 lead. Malvern's Warren Byrne scored on a deflection to tie the game 2-2. Mt. Lebanon's Eric Sloan and Malvern's Warren Byrne traded goals to make the score 3-3 midway through the final period. The Friars' Nick Averona and Keith Ennis found Tim Horn, who buried a wrist shot to give Malvern Prep a 4-3 win and the first title for coach John Graves. (Courtesy of Malvern Prep Hockey.)

Peters Township coach Mark Cooper took a gamble to start Shane Frey as opposed to Rob Madore. The teams traded goals as Gerry Raymond scored for Peters, and John Piotrowicz scored for Carroll. Eric Tangradi banged home a rebound of a Chamness shot to give Archbishop Carroll a 2-1 lead. Dustin Roux pounced on the rebound and tied the game at 2-2, and then Piotrowicz gave Archbishop Carroll a 3-2 lead, extended when Shane Aldinger beat Madore to make it 4-2. The defense shut the door in the third to give the Patriots their first title in 23 years. (Courtesy of Archbishop Carroll Hockey.)

Radnor made its third consecutive trip to the finals. Chris Brennan scored twice, and Eddie Devine added another to give Radnor a 3-0 lead. Serra's Justin Lubasch and Ray Gillis scored in the second period as the Serra Eagles cut it to 3-2. Austin Cohen beat Timmy Johnson to give Radnor a huge insurance goal and a 4-2 lead, and Colby Cohen scored for an impressive Radnor victory and the second consecutive crown for coach Ed Ritti III. (Courtesy of EPIHA.)

Malvern won the Flyers Cup in 2005, defeating Germantown in the final, 4-3. Bethel Park upended North Allegheny 1-0 in a classic Penguins Cup before 2,700-plus fans with stellar goaltending by Bryce Merriam and a goal by Tim O'Brien. In the 2005 championship, Bethel took a 2-0 lead on Jacobus Bliek and Conner McLean goals. Malvern rallied as Matt Campanale and Geoff Mucha scored to tie the game 2-2. After Malvern's Campanale and Bethel's Michael Diethorn traded goals, Kenny Lehman scored on a breakaway to give Bethel Park a 4-3 victory and its fifth state championship in eight years. (Courtesy of PIHL.)

Penncrest won its first Flyers Cup defeating Central Bucks West 6-2. Bishop McCort entered the game with five state titles. The Crimson Crushers' Cory Mock and Zac Seidel scored for a 2-0 lead. Dave Bixler scored twice to tie the game 2-2. Nick Kusturiss gave Penncrest the lead, and McCort's Marc Domonkos tied it at 3-3. Brad Ryan scored on a wrist shot early in the second to give Penncrest a 4-3 lead. Kevin Vanaman added the empty-net goal with 44 seconds left to give the Penncrest Lions their first title. (Courtesy of Penncrest Hockey.)

Haverford won the Flyers Cup, beating Council Rock South 5-1 in the finals. Peters Township knocked off Pine Richland 6-2 in the Penguins Cup. The Indians' Dustin Roux gave Peters the lead, 1-0. Bryan Papciak snapped a pass from freshman brother Chris to make it 2-0. Gerry Raymond and Dustin Roux added goals to make the final 4-0. Peters won its third championship in four years in a dominating performance. Goaltender Rob Madore earned the shutout for Peters Township. (Courtesy of PIHL.)

Mt. Lebanon went 25-0-0 and yielded only nine shots to North Allegheny, winning its fourth Penguins Cup. Cardinal O'Hara captured the Flyers Cup by defeating Germantown Academy 6-3. After Mike Censio gave O'Hara the opening goal, Shane Ferguson scored twice, and Sean McDermott another to extend the lead to 3-1. Tyler Murovich scored the clincher with a slapshot under the crossbar to make it 4-1. After Cardinal O'Hara's Tom Newman scored, Josh Mandic outraced the O'Hara player to the puck for an empty netter to give Lebo a 5-2 victory and a perfect 26-0-0 season for coach Paul Taibi. (Courtesy of Mt. Lebanon Hockey.)

Haverford High captured a second consecutive Flyers Cup with a 4-0 victory over Central Bucks South. Pine Richland pummeled Kittanning 8-3 to capture its first Penguins Cup. Goaltenders Jason Hazleton of Haverford and Stoney Hildreth of Pine Richland battled through the second period and into the third in the state final scoreless until Joe Christman's shot gave the Rams a 1-0 lead. Phil DiDinato jammed home a rebound to give the Rams a 2-0 lead. Brendan Conlon provided an empty-net goal with 1:16 remaining to seal the victory and a state championship for Pine Richland and coach Jimmy Black. (Courtesy of Pine Richland Hockey.)

The Penncrest Lions beat Springfield in the 2006 Flyers Cup, 1-0. Quaker Valley defeated Serra Catholic 6-0 to capture the Penguins Cup. Penncrest and Quaker Valley played before a packed house at Robert Morris University. The Quakers seized control of the game early on, as Furman South scored in the opening minute and brother Colin South scored twice to give the Quakers a 3-0 lead after one period. Colin South completed the hat trick, and Furman added a natural hat trick. Mikhail Lemieux and John Chicots added goals in a 9-2 final. (Courtesy of Quaker Valley Hockey.)

Haverford won three consecutive Flyers Cup championships. Pine Richland was 20-1-1, and Bobby Kennedy's club defeated Thomas Jefferson to capture its second straight Penguins Cup. Pine Richland opened up the game early and raced to a 4-0 lead on goals led by George Saad (with a pair), Dylan Trombetta, and Eric Febert. Haverford rallied in the second period as T.J. Haeberle scored a pair of goals. The teams traded goals as Matt Lohman and Phil Trombetta scored for Pine Richland, and Shane Coyle and Jimmy Hazleton scored for Haverford. Reed Loney and George Saad added goals to make the final 8-6. (Courtesy of PIHL.)

West Chester Henderson was looking to capture its first state title in 25 years for head coach Art Marcellus in 2007. Freeport shocked Quaker Valley in the Penguins Cup finals, 4-1. After a scoreless opening period, West Chester Henderson seized the lead as Billy Latta scored twice, and T.J. Wallace added another to give Henderson a 3-0 lead. Freeport's Jeremy Hepler scored inside the post to break the shutout of Rob Mattern with 41 seconds to go and make the final count 4-1 as the Warriors captured their first Class A title since 1982. (Courtesy of EPIHA.)

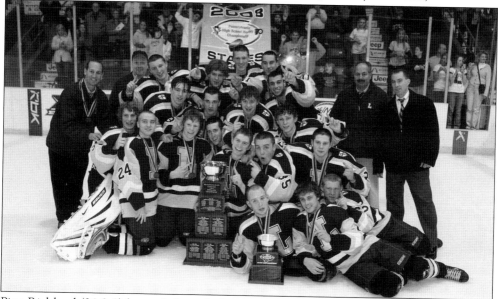

Pine Richland (24-0-0) breezed through the Penguins Cup playoffs in 2008 and took care of Meadville and Bethel Park as expected. LaSalle (29-1-2) earned a Flyers Cup victory over Holy Ghost Prep. LaSalle came out in this contest and took control; Matt O'Brien and Adam Schmidt gave LaSalle a 2-0 lead. Kyle Zoldy and Ryan Tyson scored to extend the lead to 4-0. Adam Berkle scored twice, and Adam Schmidt scored a shorthanded goal, making it 7-0. The Rams' Reed Loney scored Pine Richland's only goal in the second period, but this one was over, as the LaSalle Explorers earned the championship. (Courtesy of LaSalle Hockey.)

Conestoga (21-5-1) coach Mike Graves led the Pioneers to the 2008 Flyers Cup with a triple-overtime thriller over Pennridge 3-2 with a Vince Masciantonio goal. The Latrobe (22-3-0) head coach Ron Makoski led the Wildcats over Franklin Regional 3-2 in overtime to win their first Penguins Cup. After the scoreless opening period, Latrobe's Alex Stahl and Zack LaDuke scored to make it 2-0 Wildcats. Conestoga's Rich Masciantonio cut the lead to 2-1. Latrobe's JeffJoe Regula scored to give Latrobe a 3-1 lead. Adrian Piwonski scored to cut the lead to 3-2, but Latrobe earned its first title. (Courtesy of PIHL.)

Quaker Valley (23-2-0) entered the 2008 Class A Pennsylvania Cup after defeating Mars to capture the Penguins Cup. West Chester East (19-7-0) defeated rivals Henderson and Bayard Rustin to win the Flyers Cup. In the final, Noah Zamagias and Colin South scored to give Quaker Valley a 2-1 lead. Alex Cruit scored for West Chester East, who came alive as Mike Loughlin tied the game at two apiece. The Flyers Cup hero Steve Oriente found a loose puck and fired it home to give the Vikings a 3-2 lead with 48 seconds left, winning West Chester East the championship. (Courtesy of EPIHA.)

Shaler (23-2-0) won its first Penguins Cup in 38 years. LaSalle (25-9-5) won the title in 2008 for coach Wally Muehlbronner. In the final, the teams traded goals, as Dan Merenich and Ross Denczi scored for LaSalle, and Brian Stein and Drew Martz scored for Shaler. Martz scored to give Shaler the lead 3-2. LaSalle seized as Ross Denczi, Matt Catanese, and Mark Schnupp scored to extend the lead to 5-3. Drew Martz completed the hat trick to pull Shaler to within one, 5-4. Ross Denczi scored to make it 6-4, and LaSalle was able to repeat as state champions. (Courtesy of EPIHA.)

In the 2009 season, Latrobe (25-0-0) was in pursuit of a perfect season. Council Rock South (19-5-1) beat rival North Penn to win its first Flyers Cup. In the final, Council Rock's Peter Malamud scored to give the Hawks a 1-0 lead. The Wildcats' Matthew Batis tied the game 1-1. Latrobe came out flying in the third period as Dillon Hunter and Tyler Berger scored to extend the lead to 3-1. The Wildcats held off Council Rock South the rest of the way for a 3-2 win, and Latrobe won its second state championship. (Courtesy of PIHL.)

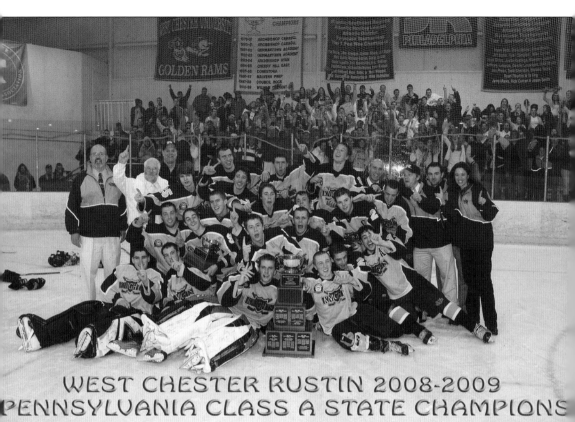

WEST CHESTER RUSTIN 2008-2009
PENNSYLVANIA CLASS A STATE CHAMPIONS

Bayard Rustin (23-2-0) matched up against Mars (23-1-0), winners of their first Penguins Cup. Rustin's Eric Knodel gained the blue line of the Mars zone and fired a laser to the stick side of Tyler Stepke to give the Knights a 1-0 lead. The Knights seized control of this state final in the second as Matt Capone, Mike Ignatuk, and William Gaffney scored to make it 4-0 after two. Phillipp Allmaier turned away all 28 shots to earn a shutout, and Brian Christie scored for a 5-0 final as Rustin earned a state title. (Courtesy of Bayard Rustin Hockey.)

Five

THE 2010s CHAMPIONSHIPS

The Penguins Cup and Flyers Cup tournaments continued to gain prestige. The Penguins Cup was competed for at the Consol Energy Arena, home of the Pittsburgh Penguins, and moved in 2014 to the Mario Lemieux Training Facility. The Flyers Cup was not be outdone, moving to the Wells Fargo Arena, home of the Philadelphia Flyers. The 2010s saw several runs of championships, as West Chester Bayard Rustin built a dynasty at the Class A level, winning six consecutive championships. LaSalle continued its assault on the Class AAA level, winning three more times in the decade to run its total to six. Peters Township stretched its championship total to five with a pair of titles. The championships were halted in 2020; for the first time since 1978, no champions were crowned. Having said that, the championships are at an all-time high, with the prestigious Flyers Cup, Penguins Cup, and Pennsylvania Cup boasting the names of 117 championship teams since 1975, including players, coaches, and managers. (Courtesy of EPIHA.)

Canon-McMillan's overtime magic finally ran out. The Big Macs beat No. 1 Shaler and No. 4 Seneca Valley to capture the Penguins Cup. The law of averages caught up to them in a 4-3 double overtime loss to Cardinal O'Hara in state championship at Mellon Arena. The clock struck midnight when the game clock showed 8:47 remaining in the second overtime. That was when the Lions' Stephen Falcone scored his second goal of the game, lifting a shot underneath the crossbar over Big Mac goalie Brandon Smolarek's glove. (Courtesy of EPIHA.)

Latrobe was a dominant team in 2010, capturing its third straight Penguins Cup 6-5 over West Allegheny. The Downingtown East Cougars won the Flyers Cup 4-2 over Council Rock South. Jayson Angus scored twice and Zach LaDuke once, and LaDuke set up Angus for the winning goal with 6:28 left in the third period as Latrobe won its third consecutive Pennsylvania Cup with a 3-2 victory against Downingtown East (24-1-1). Freshman Shane Brudnok made 32 saves for Latrobe (21-3-1). (Courtesy of PIHL.)

Bayard Rustin (13-9-2) and Mars (24-2) battled for the second consecutive year in the 2010 final. Mars won its second straight Penguins Cup over Serra Catholic, 4-1, and Bayard Rustin won its second-straight Flyers Cup 4-1 over Springfield. Tyler Stepke made 35 saves, and Robbie Sigurdsson scored twice and added an assist as Mars won its first state title 4-1 over Bayard Rustin at Mellon Arena. Stepke stopped 15 shots within the game's first 10 minutes, and Mars killed off seven Knights power plays. Brian Christie scored for Rustin. (Courtesy of PIHL.)

Upper St. Clair (16-6-1) won the Penguins Cup, defeating Fox Chapel. LaSalle (23-5-2) was looking for its fourth state title. LaSalle's Nick Popoff got a rebound to give the Explorers a 1-0 lead. The Panthers went ahead on two goals by C.J. Murray, 2-1. LaSalle Sean Orlando knotted the score 2-2. Stephen Gierlarowski gave his team a 3-2 lead. LaSalle rallied as Ron Greco scored with 2:54 to play, and the game was tied again 3-3. In overtime, C.J. Murray found the loose puck and buried it at 4:31 to give Upper St. Clair its third state title. (Courtesy of PIHL.)

The Council Rock South Golden Hawks (24-4-1) defeated Central Bucks East 5-2 in the Flyers Cup. Canevin (19-4-0) won the Penguins Cup over Peters Township, 5-2. The Hawks' Zack Goodman scored on a rebound to give Council Rock South a 1-0 lead. Canevin's Nick Hart scored from the doorstep to tie the game at 1-1. Matt Walsh scored to give the Crusaders a 2-1 lead. Matt Walsh scored into an empty net with 59 seconds to give Canevin a 3-1 win and a fourth state title for the Crusaders. (Courtesy of PIHL.)

The Springfield Cougars (17-5-3) defeated Unionville 3-2 in overtime to capture their second Flyers Cup Class A crown. The Mars Planets (23-1-0) earned the state final, defeating upstart Hampton in the Penguins Cup, 5-0. Nick Blaney found a wide-open net to give the Planets a 1-0 lead. Springfield's Dave Allen scored on a bang-bang play to tie it 1-1. Elliott Tisdale scored on a backhand to give a 2-1 lead to Mars. Nick Blaney, Austin Heakins, and Elliott Tisdale scored to make it 5-1. Springfield's Connor Phillips scored to make it a 5-2 final, and Mars captured its second-straight title. (Courtesy of PIHL.)

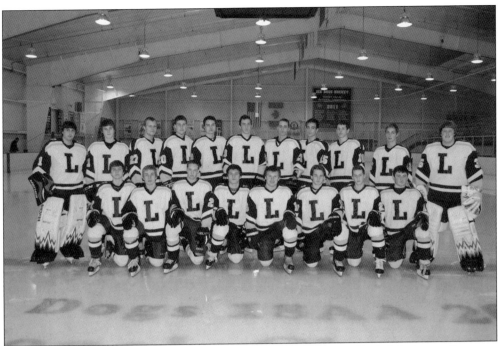

LaSalle has been to the state final four out of the past five years. Bethel Park won five state championships and reeled off 15 straight to win the 2012 Penguins Cup. LaSalle defeated Holy Ghost Prep in the Flyers Cup and Bethel Park 6-2 in the final. LaSalle's Andrew Grajewski scored twice, and Andrew Romano, Matt Williams, Nick Master, and Brett Supinski each scored once. Senior goalie Andrew King stopped 25 of the 27 shots he faced. (Courtesy of EPIHA.)

Council Rock South made its third trip to the finals. West Allegheny overcame Cathedral Prep 4-3 in an overtime contest for its first Penguins Cup. The Indians held leads of 1-0, 2-1, and 3-2 during the first two periods. The Golden Hawks led just once, but it was when the final buzzer sounded, and they skated off with a 4-3 win and a state title. Just 46 seconds into the third, Paul Cloud scored to tie the game, and six minutes later, Cloud found Ufberg, who fired a wrist shot past West Allegheny goalie Jason Kumpfmiller for the game-winner. (Courtesy of EPIHA.)

Bayard Rustin won 15 games in a row and swept through the Flyers Cup. Quaker Valley defeated Mars in the Penguins Cup final. Bayard Rustin scored 30 seconds in, but Quaker Valley controlled play the rest of the way and won its second state championship 4-1. Rustin's Jeff Nelson scored for the Knights. Kevin Kenny beat Bayard Rustin goalie Zach Sheriko for a score of 1-1. Clayton Bouchard, Ryan Lottes, and Otto Schaefer also scored for Quaker Valley (21-1-1). Doug Revak stopped 16 of 17 shots for the Quakers. (Courtesy of PIHL.)

In the Penguins Cup against Peters Township, Joe Griffin scored twice as the North Allegheny Tigers won 2-0. LaSalle won the Flyers Cup five of the past six years. LaSalle built a 2-0 lead in the first period. The Tigers responded in the second period with a natural hat trick by Joe Griffin to take a 3-2 lead. In the third period, Joe Griffin set up Dominic Zangaro to make it 4-2. North Allegheny goaltender Bradford Thornburgh stopped 34 of 36 shots, and Matt Fantaski and Griffin added empty netters, making the final 6-2 and giving North Allegheny its second title. (Courtesy of PIHL.)

Cherokee earned a place in the Flyers Cup final and defeated Parkland in the Flyers Cup 6-3. Since Cherokee is from New Jersey, the team was ineligible for the Pennsylvania final. In the Penguins Cup final against Pine Richland, the Wildcats' Dan Staffen, Dalton Hunter (twice), Adam Ferguson, and Brendan Johns scored in a 5-0 win. Latrobe outshot Parkland 41-9 and scored four unanswered goals to win its fourth AA crown 4-1. Dalton Hunter scored twice, and Chris Johnson and Adam Ferguson added goals for the Wildcats. (Courtesy of PIHL.)

Quaker Valley captured its fourth Penguins Cup over Mars. West Chester East won the Flyers Cup over Springfield 7-3. Zach Higgins and Jesse Abarca scored twice as the Vikings built a 5-1 lead and held on to win a second Class A title for West Chester East. Quaker Valley rallied for four goals in the third period as Connor Quinn and Jimmy Perkins scored two goals each. The Quakers' 46-game winning streak was snapped. (Courtesy of EPIHA.)

Peters Township captured its fifth Penguins Cup title, beating Bethel Park 4-2. LaSalle has become one of Pennsylvania's storied hockey programs since winning the AAA crown four times in 1998 (Central Catholic), 2008 (Pine Richland), 2009 (Shaler), and 2012 (Bethel Park) for coach Wally Muehlbronner. Peters Township's Brian Baker stopped 31 shots, and Kittelberger scored the winning goal as the Indians (20-4) claimed the Class AAA Pennsylvania Cup with a 2-1 victory against La Salle College (18-10-2). Adam Alavi and Joel Kittelberger scored for Peters. (Courtesy of PIHL.)

Central Bucks South beat Souderton 5-2 to win its first Flyers Cup. Canevin beat Cathedral Prep 1-0 in the Penguins Cup final. Canevin (23-2) could not overcome a lack of offense in a 5-2 loss to Central Bucks South (19-3-1) in the state final. Leo Flick scored twice, and Brendan Clements, Michael Pilla, and Michael Lucas scored for the Titans. Liam Walsh and Randy Unger scored for Canevin. Coach Tom Coyne led his team to its first state championship. (Courtesy of EPIHA.)

Quaker Valley's Connor Quinn scored four times as his team beat Thomas Jefferson in an 8-2 Penguins Cup win. Bayard Rustin won its fourth Flyers Cup in 2014 over Springfield, 4-1. Bayard Rustin (20-3-2) led 4-1 after one period and went on to beat Quaker Valley (24-2) 5-2 to win the state title. Brett Christie, Michael Grande, and J.R. Barone (with a pair) scored to give Rustin a 4-1 lead, and Shawn Polidore put the game away with a late third period goal. Jimmy Perkins and Cameron Peterkin scored for the Quakers. (Courtesy of EPIHA.)

Veteran Holy Ghost Prep coach Gump Whiteside won a Flyers Cup title over La Salle, 6-3. Canon McMillan won its second Penguins Cup and first since 2010 by defeating Butler 4-0 at Consol Energy Center. Nicholas Bohatiuk scored four goals and had an assist as Holy Ghost Prep captured the Pennsylvania Cup Class AAA title by beating Canon-McMillan 6-4 at Penn State. Kyle Peters rounded out the scoring for the Firebirds, netting two goals in the second period. Peters also earned an assist on Bohatiuk's final score. (Courtesy of EPIHA.)

Cathedral Prep (20-2-0) and Downingtown East (14-7-2) met for the Pennsylvania AA title. Cathedral Prep captured the Penguins Cup over Armstrong 3-2 in the final. Downingtown East defeated North Penn 4-1 in the Flyers Cup. Downingtown East scored the opening goal from Ben Robertson. Dillon Elliott tied the game, and Jack Kelly gave the Ramblers the lead, 2-1. Hunter Emerson added an insurance goal as Cathedral Prep held off the Cougars to win its third Pennsylvania title under head coach Craig Barnett, 3-1 over Downingtown East. The final shots were Cathedral Prep 32, Downingtown East 17. (Courtesy of PIHL.)

West Chester Rustin 2015 States A Champions

Mars and Bayard Rustin met in 2009 and 2010, splitting the first two meetings. Mars repeated in 2011, and Rustin in 2014. Mars defeated Quaker Valley in the Penguins Cup. Bayard Rustin led 1-0 as Tommy Sloan scored and Mars tied the game via Paul Maust. In the third, Mars took the lead as Kyle Thomas scored. Rustin tied the game as Eric Flynn beat Mars goaltender Tyler Spreng. The Knights took the lead as Brett Christie and Michael Grande scored to make it 4-2. Grande added an empty netter to make it 5-2. Jason Grande stopped 40 Mars shots. (Courtesy of Bayard Rustin Hockey.)

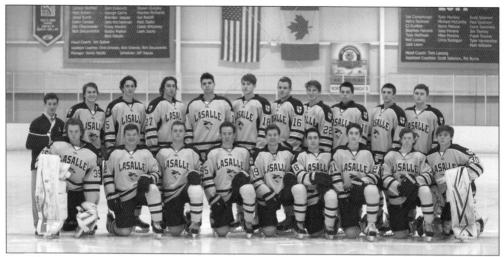

LaSalle captured its record-breaking ninth Flyers Cup over Holy Ghost Prep. Coach Wally Muehlbronner's club has been to the state finals eight times, winning Pennsylvania high school hockey's ultimate hockey prize in 1998, 2008, 2009, and 2012. Cathedral Prep won its fourth Penguins Cup by defeating North Allegheny 4-3 in overtime. La Salle defeated Erie Cathedral Prep 7-1 at the state championship. Senior goalie Harrison Feeney stopped 25 shots for the win, while Henry Kaechelin, Coty Thomas, Joe Mancuso, David Mester, Austin Master, and Tyler Pohlig scored to lead the offense. (Courtesy of EPIHA.)

The 2016 state championship was a rematch of the 2014 state final between Central Bucks South and Canevin. Canevin won its eighth Penguins Cup, defeating Mars. Central Bucks South, under Tom Coyne, won the Flyers Cup over Downingtown East, 3-2. Central Bucks South dominated Canevin from the outset with a 7-3 win. Matt Stoll propelled Central Bucks South as he netted four goals. The Titans took complete command over the final three minutes of the frame to make the score 6-2. In the third period, the sides exchanged goals as the Titans won their second title in three years. (Courtesy of EPIHA.)

Franklin Regional won the Penguins Cup final against South Fayette with four third-period goals and its first Penguins Cup in seven tries, 4-1. Bayard Rustin has collected six Flyers Cups and three state titles in their short history. The Knights defeated rivals West Chester East in the Flyers Cup. Golden Knights forward Matt Owens had the hat trick, Brett Christie chipped in two goals and an assist, and junior netminder Jason Grande stopped 22 shots as Bayard Rustin (20-3-2) won its third consecutive state title 6-0 against first-time finalist Franklin Regional (19-7-0). (Courtesy of EPIHA.)

Peters Township endured a 10-8-2 regular season, and in the Penguins Cup final, rattled off three unanswered goals to capture its sixth Penguins Cup 5-2 over Central Catholic. Peters Township would not be denied in the state finals, as Sam Barnes scored a power play goal in the game's waning moments and freshman goaltender Alex Wilbert held off a rally from Flyers Cup champions Holy Ghost Prep to win 2-1 and give the program its sixth state title. (Courtesy of PIHL.)

Plum won the Penguins Cup over Latrobe. Downingtown East beat William Tennent in the Flyers Cup, 8-3. In the state final, Downingtown East's Justin Cohn scored to give the Cougars a 1-0 lead. Cougar senior Jonathan Carreiro scored to put Downingtown East ahead 2-0. Plum scored its lone goal, tallied by Nolan Puhala. Downingtown East regained its two-goal lead when junior Luca Pisani scored on the power play and Downingtown East led 3-1. The Cougars shut down Plum the rest of the way and picked up their first state title. (Courtesy of EPIHA.)

Bayard Rustin entered the 2017 playoffs looking to become the third program in state history to earn four consecutive titles, after Meadville and Bishop McCort. Rustin defeated West Chester East in four overtimes. Franklin Regional beat Indiana for a rematch with Rustin. The Knights fell behind Penguins Cup champions Franklin Regional as Jamie Mauro scored for the Panthers. Rustin tied the contest as Brett Turner scored in the second period. In overtime, after Jason Grande stopped Franklin's Olda Virag, the Knights' Matt Owens scored the game-winner to give Bayard Rustin their fourth straight title. (Courtesy of EPIHA.)

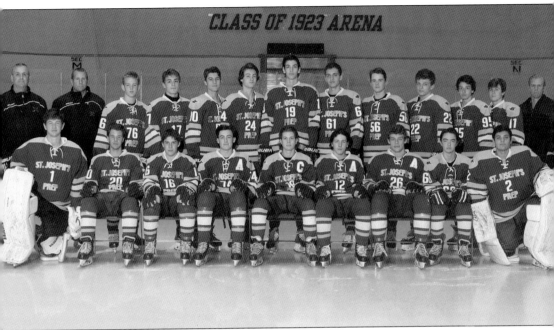

CLASS OF 1923 ARENA

St. Joseph's Prep has been knocking on the Flyers Cup door for the past five years under head coach David Giacomin. St. Joe's won the Flyers Cup for the first time by defeating Holy Ghost Prep. Seneca Valley beat Peters Township to capture its first Penguins Cup. Marc Colavita scored three times, and Tyler Boucher added an unassisted power play goal to lift Flyers Cup champion Saint Joseph's Prep to a victory over Penguins Cup champion Seneca Valley 4-0 in the state title game at Ice Line Rink in West Chester. Seneca Valley was outshot 34-19. (Courtesy of EPIHA.)

The Armstrong hockey program waited 27 years to return to the Class AA state title game. Upon arrival, it had to wait again, through eight periods and more than 90 minutes of hockey, before a winner could be declared at Ice Line Quad Rinks in West Chester. Downingtown East claimed its second consecutive championship 3-2 on Ryan Prestayko's goal 2:34 into the fifth overtime. Luca Pisani and Jack Barton also scored for Downingtown East, and Easton Hooks and Jacob Gross scored for Armstrong as the teams battled 2-2 in regulation. (Courtesy of EPIHA.)

Bishop McCort was able to defeat Meadville in a thriller overtime game and capture its first Penguins Cup in 13 years. Bayard Rustin has won four consecutive state titles under Nick Russo, looking for its sixth championship. Nicholas Ferraro had two goals, and Ian Strasinski and Justin Demyan added goals as Flyers Cup champion Bayard Rustin won the Class A Pennsylvania Cup 3-1 at Ice Line Rink in West Chester. Joel Keller made 22 saves to secure the win. Brett Seitz scored for Bishop McCort. (Courtesy of EPIHA.)

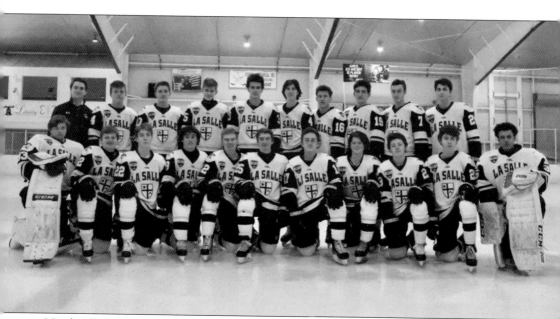

North Allegheny captured the Penguins Cup 3-0 over Peters Township. LaSalle ousted defending champs St. Joe's in the Flyers Cup. North Allegheny and LaSalle battled through two periods to a 3-3 tie as Aaron Miller scored twice for North Allegheny. The Tigers had a point-blank opportunity blocked and cleared, and La Salle's Sam Lipkin stole the puck and scored on goalie Richard Karapandi, who slipped trying to get into position. Lipkin's goal turned out to be the game winner, and La Salle added two late empty-net goals to secure a 6-3 win over North Allegheny. (Courtesy of EPIHA.)

Downingtown East won the Flyers Cup with a 7-2 victory over Downingtown West. Pine Richland captured its fourth Penguins Cup with a 7-5 victory over Upper St. Clair. The Rams got an early lead and never looked back en route to defeating two-time defending state champion Downingtown East 3-0 in the final. Junior goaltender Daniel Stauffer stopped all 24 shots on the net to preserve the shutout. The Rams scored when senior Brian Phipps found the back of the net. In the second period, the Rams' William Studt scored on a wrister. Pine Richland (22-0-1) captured its first state championship since 2007. (Courtesy of PIHL.)

The Montour Spartans had a dream season and captured the school's first Penguins Cup, defeating the South Fayette team in the finals 6-3. The West Chester Rustin Knights won their sixth consecutive Pennsylvania Cup and seventh state title with a dominant 11-3 victory over Montour. The Knights raced to a 6-0 lead paced by a Matt Owens hat trick with Nick Ferraro assisting on three first-period tallies. Rustin added on, scoring four more goals to make the lopsided final result. The Knights won the state title in six title seasons and seven times overall. (Courtesy of EPIHA.)

Six

TOP 10 GAMES IN CHAMPIONSHIP HISTORY

The Pennsylvania high school hockey championships have evolved into a full-weekend event. The state title has been contested at the AAA and AA levels for 45 years and the Class A level since 1989. How schools are classified has varied over the years, but the consistent theme has been that Class AAA is large enrollment, and Class A is smaller enrollment, based on the number of male students. Regardless, the Flyers Cup and Penguins Cup now crown champions at AAA, AA, and A, and the winners meet for the state championship. Over the years, there have been many memorable games and moments. The 10 games described in this chapter have left a mark on the state final that add to the prestige and honor when students from schools in Eastern and Western Pennsylvania convene every spring to try to earn the title of champions. (Courtesy of Downingtown East Hockey.)

Baldwin enjoyed a 20-4-2 regular season qualifying for the first Pennsylvania high school hockey championships. The Highlanders defeated Erie McDowell 4-3 and Springfield 2-1 in overtime to earn a spot in the first state final. They faced rival Churchill, and the teams battled to a 3-3 tie through regulation. Jim Cox's overtime goal at 1:10 of the extra session gave Baldwin the first state championship in Pennsylvania with a 4-3 win over the Chargers. Goaltender Brad Allman and Cox were named to the all-tournament team. Verne Shaver scored a pair of goals for Churchill. (Courtesy of the Pennsylvania Hockey Foundation Archives.)

Abington and Gateway swept through the round-robin with three wins to set up the state final. Gateway was led by University of Denver recruit John Liprando. In the state championship game, Abington's Mark Leegard scored first. Gateway rallied on goals by Tom Miller and Rick Fitchwell. The Ghosts rallied to take the lead 3-2 in the third period, setting up a heroic goal by Liprando with 16 seconds left. Abington won in overtime as Dennis Garvin scored on a power play with 51 seconds remaining to give the Ghosts the title, handing Gateway its first loss of the season. (Courtesy of the Pennsylvania Hockey Foundation Archives.)

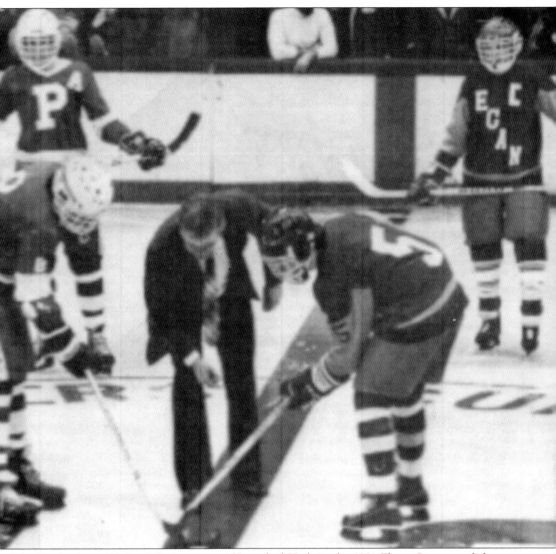

The Patriots' convincing 9-0 victory over Haverford High in the 1981 Flyers Cup earned them a spot in the final against western champions North Catholic, which gained a spot with a 3-1 victory over 1980 champions Upper St. Clair. Archbishop Carroll had a 26-2-0 record, and North Catholic was undefeated. In the final, Archbishop Carroll edged North Catholic 4-3 in a thriller. North Catholic trailed the entire game and rallied from a two-goal deficit twice but was unable to gain the equalizer. The Patriots became the first Philadelphia area school to win the state crown. (Courtesy of EPIHA.)

The Panthers marched through the 1986-1987 regular season undefeated at 22-0-0. Upper St. Clair continued its dominance of Western Pennsylvania hockey in the playoffs, defeating Westmont Hilltop, Erie Cathedral Prep, and rivals Mt. Lebanon in the Penguins Cup. In the state final, the Panthers faced Flyers Cup champions Malvern Prep, and it took an overtime goal by Chris Wittemore to defeat the Friars. The win in the final capped a perfect season for Upper St. Clair to match the undefeated season of 1986 AAA champs Conestoga. (Courtesy of EPIHA.)

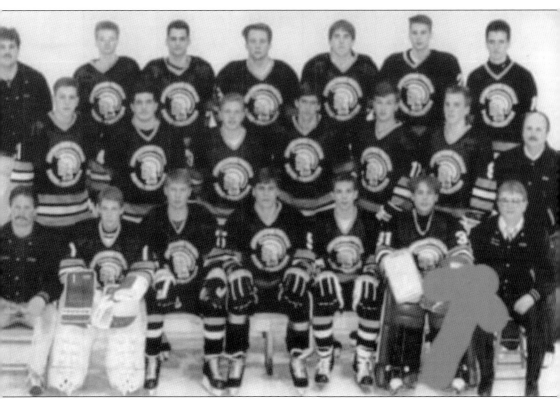

Father Judge earned a berth in the final by defeating West Chester East. Johnstown captured a berth with a Penguins Cup win over Chartiers Valley, 8-4. In the final, Father Judge raced to a 5-1 lead after two periods. Johnstown rallied behind a pair of goals each by Brian Bunn and Brian Wincer to tie the game with 1:17 remaining. Father Judge got the game winner with just four seconds on the clock, and Mike Bill scored on a rebound to give the Crusaders their first championship with a 6-5 victory over the Trojans before 1,500 fans. (Courtesy of Johnstown High School Hockey.)

In the state final, Meadville and Conwell Egan played before a packed house. Conwell Egan took leads of 1-0 and 2-1 on goals by Nick Caruso and Mitch LaFleur into the third period. Meadville, on goals from Nick Tucci and Ryan Minik, tied the game. Meadville outshot Egan 52-45 into the third overtime. Goaltenders Tomas Mikus and Matt Cusanno were terrific as both teams had quality chances to win the game. At 2:10 of the third overtime, Brian Tetley fired home a wrist shot to the stick side to give the Eagles their third title, 3-2. (Courtesy of Alvina Tetley.)

Bethel Park and Malvern Prep met in the final for the third time. After the teams played to a 1-1 tie through two and a half periods, Malvern's Michael Curran found a rebound and gave Malvern the lead with 1:58 to go in regulation. Bethel Park's Tony Sands tied the game with 1:34 remaining and sent it to overtime at 2-2. In overtime, C.J. Strauss took a long shot, and a cutting Justin Glock got the tip of his stick on it to send it past Sorenstrom, giving Bethel Park its third straight state championship. (Courtesy of the Pennsylvania Hockey Foundation Archives.)

Canon-McMillan's overtime magic finally ran out. The Big Macs beat Shaler and Seneca Valley to capture the Penguins Cup. The law of averages caught up to them in a 4-3 double-overtime loss to Cardinal O'Hara in the Pennsylvania Cup championship game at Mellon Arena. The clock struck midnight when the Mellon Arena game clock showed 8:47 remaining in the second overtime. That is when the Lions' Stephen Falcone scored his second goal of the game, lifting a shot underneath the crossbar on Big Mac goalie Brandon Smolarek's glove side, just inside the left post. (Courtesy of the Pittsburgh *Post-Gazette*.)

In a rematch of the 2016 final, the Knights fell behind Penguins Cup champions Franklin Regional as Jamie Mauro scored for the Panthers. Rustin tied the contest as Brett Turner scored in the second period. In a classic goaltending duel between Franklin Regional's Danny Soltesz and Bayard Rustin's Jason Grande, the game headed to overtime. Franklin Regional had several great chances, but the Knights' Matt Owens notched the game-winner to give Bayard Rustin its fourth straight state title in 2017. Jason Grande and Tommy Sloan made Pennsylvania hockey history as players capturing four consecutive state titles. (Courtesy of the Pittsburgh *Tribune-Review*.)

Armstrong waited 27 years to return to the state title game. Upon arrival, it had to wait again, through eight periods and more than 90 minutes of hockey, before a winner could be declared. It seemed especially cruel to the Riverhawks when that winner was Downingtown East, claiming its second consecutive Class AA championship 3-2 on Ryan Prestayko's goal 2:34 into the fifth overtime. Both goalies turned in yeoman efforts: Armstrong's Bowser turned away 43 shots, and Matt Shandler had 50 saves for Downingtown East. (Courtesy of PIHL.)

Seven

Top 10 Teams

Any list of the top 10 teams over nearly 45 years of Pennsylvania high school hockey championships must necessarily leave out some outstanding teams. The honorable-mention list is rounded out by many memorable teams that left their mark on history. These teams include the 1979 Churchill squad; Meadville in 1992, 1993, and 1995; LaSalle in 2016; and Bayard Rustin in 2019. These teams were all under strong consideration for this chapter. The teams that round out the top 25 include 1983 Germantown Academy, 1984 Canevin, 1995 and 1996 Bishop McCort, 1997 Cathedral Prep, 2000 Thomas Jefferson, 2004 Malvern Prep, 2004 Radnor, and 2006 Quaker Valley. All were certainly top-10 worthy, but fell a little short. While all of these schools and teams were very impressive, this chapter explores the 10 most elite Pennsylvania high school hockey teams of all time. (Courtesy of EPIHA.)

Churchill was a great hockey program in the early days of high school hockey in Pennsylvania, and while the 1975 and 1976 teams made it to the state finals, the 1977 team was able to capture the title with an undefeated regular season against the stern competition in the WPIHL AAA division. This team had depth with four lines, strong defense and goaltending, and an outstanding coach in Dan Sheehy, who capture a second state title in 1979. (Courtesy of the Pennsylvania Hockey Foundation Archives.)

Archbishop Carroll enjoyed a great run from 1978 to 1981 in the early days of Pennsylvania high school hockey, winning three ICSHL titles and two Flyers Cup championships. The Patriots had many travel players from the Little Flyers organization. Carroll was by far the premier program in Eastern Pennsylvania and defeated the champions of the ICSHL, LBCSHL, EHSHL, and SHSHL to capture the Flyers Cup. In defeating Western Pennsylvania's top team North Catholic in the 1981 state final, the Patriots ensured their place among the state's finest teams. (Courtesy of EPIHA.)

Conestoga won the 1985 state championship defeating Penguins Cup champions Mt. Lebanon. Coach Taylor Railton led Conestoga to an undefeated regular season in the ICSHL. The 1986 Pioneers went on to run the table and win the Flyers Cup over Malvern Prep and then defeated the Penguins Cup champions Upper St. Clair to capture the school's first state title and cap the first undefeated team in Pennsylvania high school hockey history, staking a claim as one of the state's finest teams and seasons. (Courtesy of Mike Graves.)

rsity: *Front:* Jon Hoffnagle, Jamie Gilbert, Dave asnick, Greg Krock, Chris Wittemore, Jim McVay. *ck:* Marty Owens, Chris Koon, Eric Baumgartner,

Dennis Wilson, Dean Wegner, Tim Krock, Phil S falo, Paul Schobert, Pete Shaffalo, Louis Cassa Don Slogan.

Upper St. Clair captured the state title in 1980, and the 1987 team ran through the SHIHL season with an unblemished record. The Panthers swept through the Penguins Cup playoffs in impressive fashion with wins over Western Pennsylvania top teams under coach Dave Hornack. Upper St. Clair defeated Flyers Cup champions Malvern Prep to cap an undefeated season and stake its claim as one of the greatest teams in state history. (Courtesy of Upper St. Clair Hockey.)

Meadville is by far the most storied high school hockey program in state history, with eight titles. But when trying to choose the best Meadville team, the answers are vague at best. The 1994 team was as dominant as any in Pennsylvania hockey history as the Bulldogs overwhelmed the competition in the Penguins Cup playoffs with 33 goals for and 5 against. This separates this team from many others. (Courtesy of the Pennsylvania Hockey Foundation Archives.)

BETHEL PARK HOCKEY
CHAMPIONS

PIHL

1999-2000
2000-2001
2001-2002
2002-2003

PA
STATE
1999-2000
2000-2001
2001-2002

PENGUIN
CUP
1999-2000
2000-2001
2001-2002

Bethel Park was a bridesmaid for many years until capturing the title in 1997, overcoming Meadville in the Penguins Cup and winning the state title over Malvern Prep. Under coach Jim McVay, the team showed a commitment to defense and discipline. No team exemplified this more than the 2001 squad. The Hawks yielded only 27 goals in 27 games, complemented by some excellent clutch scoring, to capture the AAA state championship in impressive fashion. This cemented their claim as one of the top 10 teams in state history. (Courtesy of the Pennsylvania Hockey Foundation Archives.)

Peters Township had a great run from 2002 to 2005, with four Penguins Cups and three state championships under Mark Cooper. The Indians' roster was loaded with NCAA Division I players and American Collegiate Hockey Association standouts, and ran the table in 2003. Peters put an exclamation point on the season, defeating Holy Ghost in the state finals with one of the most dominating performances in state history, making it an easy choice for the top 10. Holy Ghost Prep head coach Brian Tibbels called Peters "better than any AAA teams in the state." (Courtesy of the Pennsylvania Hockey Foundation Archives.)

The LaSalle hockey program has won a record 10 Flyers Cups and five state championships. The Explorers have had many great teams, but the pinnacle was in 2008, when they defeated state champions from half a dozen states and captured the Pennsylvania final in a dominating fashion against Holy Ghost Prep and Pine Richland. It was one of the most dominating teams in state history. (Courtesy of LaSalle College Prep Hockey.)

Bayard Rustin won six state titles from 2014 to 2019 under head coach Nick Russo. In the 2017 final, the Knights fell behind Penguins Cup champions Franklin Regional and headed to overtime again. Matt Owens notched the game-winner to give Bayard Rustin its fourth straight championship. The Knights won the USA Hockey national championship when Rustin beat Santa Margarita, California, 4-3 to earn a historic national championship. This team had depth in its seniors, underclassmen, and development. (Courtesy of EPIHA.)

Eight

Top 12 Coaches

Coaching high school hockey in Pennsylvania began with hockey dads who volunteered in the development of the programs in the early days. Several professional hockey players and former collegiate, junior, and high school standouts have manned the benches. This chapter presents a list of the top 12 coaches along with some honorable mentions. Right out of the gate in the early days of the Flyers Cup, Penguins Cup, and state championships, there were plenty of great leaders. Bruce Craig of Germantown Academy led the Pioneers to their first Flyers Cup in 1982, and a state championship over Bethel Park the next year. In 1984, Cathedral Prep's Nels White brought home a state title, and another in 1997. The 1990s saw a colorful, passionate coach in Greensburg Central Catholic's Butch Marrietta, who won in 1993, 1994, and 1996. Thomas Jefferson's Don Powell captured three straight Pennsylvania AA championships in 1998, 1999, and 2000. Former Serra Catholic and Colorado College player John Mooney led a scrappy Serra Catholic squad to three consecutive state titles in 2000, 2001, and 2002. Another prominent coach was Bishop Egan/Conwell Egan's Rich Slack, who guided the Eagles to state titles in 1990 at A, 1995 at AA, and one more time in 1999 at AAA. Radnor fell to Serra in the 2002 final under Ed Ritti III but went on to capture the 2003 and 2004 state titles. Quaker Valley's Kevin Quinn brought home the state title in 2006 and again in 2012. The dominance of Eastern Pennsylvania teams in the fifth decade of the Pennsylvania high school hockey championships was led by LaSalle and Bayard Rustin, with nine titles between them. Not to be outdone was Tom Coyne of Central Bucks South, who won in 2014 and 2016, and Dave Hendricks of Downingtown East High School in 2017 and 2018. (Courtesy of Mike Graves.)

Jamie Plunkett is a native of Toronto, Ontario, and played NCAA Division 1 hockey at Cornell University. He continued his journey at Meadville High School in 1987, where he has been at the helm for 33 years. He is considered by many the finest coach in the history of Pennsylvania high school hockey. As the chief of Bulldog Nation, Plunkett has accumulated eight state championships (1987, 1989, 1992–1996, 2003), nine Penguins Cup titles (1987, 1989, 1992–1996, 1999, 2003), and 10 LKSHL crowns (1987–1996, 1998). His records are unrivalled, with a 439-94-26 mark, including 380-76-26 in the regular season and 59-18 in state playoffs. Richard Holabaugh has been steadfast in support of Plunkett for a majority of his tenure with the Meadville hockey program. Former Bulldog standout Scott Phillis and his family have been instrumental in supporting Plunkett and the Meadville hockey program throughout its history. Meadville hockey was built through the Crawford County youth program. The Bulldogs annually play over 40 league and non-league games against the top competition from Pennsylvania, Ohio, New York, and Ontario to hone their playoff skills. Plunkett's record of eight state championships and nine Penguins Cups is unmatched in state history. His domination of Class AAA from 1989 through 1996 is unmatched. The Bulldogs have been the measuring stick for every high school hockey program for 33 years since 1987, all under Jamie Plunkett. (Left, courtesy of the Pennsylvania Hockey Foundation Archives; right, courtesy of Brandon Corey.)

Nick Russo is a native of West Chester and began his journey at the collegiate and amateur level, including the Keystone State Games. Coach Russo started at Bayard Rustin in 2007, and in 12 years, led the Knights to an unprecedented run in Pennsylvania high school hockey history. Russo led his school to seven state championships (2009, 2014–2019) and nine Flyers Cup titles (2009, 2010, 2012, 2014–2019). His stats in Eastern Pennsylvania hockey are unprecedented, with a 48-6 record in the playoffs. Ken Sheriko and Michael Giduck have been with Russo for the majority of his tenure with Rustin. The Bayard Rustin hockey program has taken advantage of the terrific Ice Line Quad Rinks facility in West Chester. Russo built Rustin through building grade school, middle school, junior varsity, and varsity teams. Players in the program play Tier 1 and Tier 2 competition outside the high school program while joining the Knights in their quest for the Flyers Cup in the Chesmont Division of the ICSHL AA and A. Russo's record of seven state championships, including six in a row, is legendary in Pennsylvania scholastic hockey. The Knights have combined a strong core of Tier 2 players, highlighted by many Tier 1 players who have come through the program. (Above, courtesy of Bayard Rustin Hockey; below, courtesy of the Pennsylvania Hockey Foundation Archives.)

Jimmy Black is a native of Pittsburgh and began his journey as a player for North Catholic High School and the Royal Travelers at the amateur level. He coached 14 years with Beaver, North Hills, Pine Richland, and North Allegheny High Schools. Black was instrumental in winning four state championships (1991 as assistant coach with Beaver, 2006 with Pine Richland, 2007 and 2013 with North Allegheny), and four Penguins Cup titles in the same years. His records in Western Pennsylvania hockey are 181-85-30 in the regular season and 20-10 in the playoffs. The Pine Richland and North Allegheny hockey programs were built through the number-rich programs of the North Hills of Pittsburgh. Both programs were annual contenders for the Penguins Cup, but were not able to get it over the top until 2005 when North Allegheny made it to the final but lost a heartbreaker to Bethel Park. Just a year later, under Jimmy Black, Pine Richland won its first Penguins Cup in school history and finished it off with a state title. The following year, Black led North Allegheny to its first Penguins Cup and state championship, and repeated that feat in 2013. While there are quite a few coaches who won three state championships (and a fourth as assistant coach), none did it in the manner of Jimmy Black. Pine Richland was a perennial powerhouse of talent, but Black put them over the top in 2006 and again at North Allegheny in 2007. North Allegheny's 2013 team was another encore performance, defeating a very good LaSalle team. In Black's second stint at Pine Richland, the 2019 state championship team had his handprints all over it, winning the state title over two-time champions Downingtown East. (Courtesy of PIHL.)

Jim McVay is a native of Upper St. Clair who played hockey at Upper St. Clair High School and Colby College. He began his coaching career at Bethel Park High School in 1996 and has been at the helm for 23 years. McVay also won a state title as a player with Upper St. Clair in 1987. As a coach, he won five state championships (1997 as assistant, 2000, 2001, 2002, 2005), and six Penguins Cup titles in the same years, plus 2012. His records in Western Pennsylvania hockey are 336-107-31 in the regular season and 40-18 in the playoffs. The Bethel Park program had a great history of being a perennial Penguins Cup contender in the 1980s and 1990s but could not overcome Meadville, losing to the Bulldogs in 1993, 1994, and 1995 in the finals. The Hawks made it to the 1997 final, and under Bobby Kennedy and Jim McVay, were able to break through to win the Penguins Cup and the state title over Malvern Prep. Under the leadership of McVay, Bethel went on to win four more state championships with dominant defensive teams and timely scoring. Winning five state championships in eight years puts Jim McVay and the Bethel Park program in elite company in state history. The three-year run from 2000 to 2002 showcased a dominant defensive performance, yielding just 83 goals in 83 regular season and playoff games. (Courtesy of Jim McVay.)

Galen Head was a professional hockey player for the Johnstown Chiefs, and John Bradley made his mark at Boston University prior to joining the Chiefs. Head started with Bishop McCort in 1985 and coached 11 years until 1996, when Bradley took over the reins, coaching for 23 years through the 2019-2020 season. Head and Bradley have led Bishop McCort to five state championships (1994–1997, 1999) and seven Penguins Cup championships (1994–1997, 1999, 2005, 2018). Galen Head's regular season record over 11 years was 117-95-9, with a 27-5 record in the playoffs. John Bradley has a record of 323-118-12 and 36-17 in the playoffs, for a combined record of 503-235-21. Bradley and Mike Hudec have been staples of the Bishop McCort program and carried Head's legacy from the mid-1990s through today, adding state titles in 1997 and 1999 for the Crimson Crushers. The Bishop McCort program had humble beginnings, with a winless season in 1984-1985. The Crushers have enjoyed great success through the foundation laid by Head, who was personally responsible for three state championships and three Penguins Cup titles, with five appearances in the western finals. McCort went on to become the most dominant Class A program in state history, with five state championships and seven Penguins Cup championships, adding titles in 2005 and 2018. (Courtesy of John Bradley.)

Bob Huber wandered off the football field as a youth coach in 1972 to take on a new challenge with ice hockey, and coached Churchill to a pair of state finals and four WPIHL championships. Dan Sheehy joined the staff in 1975-1976 and was well known in the amateur ranks as a tremendous development coach. He used that experience to win two state championships in 1977 and 1979 and three additional WPIHL crowns. Huber and Sheehy combined for four consecutive trips to the state championship in its first four years of existence, forming the early dynasty of high school hockey in Western Pennsylvania. With a regular season record of 162-25-8 and 29-5 in the playoffs, Churchill dominated the early days of Pennsylvania hockey. Assistant coaches Fred Mauro and Roger Artz were instrumental in developing talented players into winners. Churchill made four consecutive appearances in the state championships from 1975 to 1979, a record at the Class AAA level that was only surpassed by Malvern Prep in 2005. The 29 wins and just 5 losses in eight years in playoff games is equally impressive, as the Chargers netted seven WPIHL titles in eight years (1973–1976, 1978–1980). (Both, courtesy of the Pennsylvania Hockey Foundation Archives.)

Wally Muehlbronner is a native of Philadelphia and serves as the admissions director at LaSalle College Prep. He began his coaching career at LaSalle in 1996, and in 24 years has led the Explorers to an unprecedented run in state high school hockey, with six championships (1998, 2008, 2009, 2012, 2016, 2019) and 10 Flyers Cup championships (1996, 1998, 2008, 2009, 2011–2014, 2016, 2019). John Haggerty has been with Muehlbronner for a majority of his 24 years with LaSalle, with a record of 51-16 in the playoffs. LaSalle's 10 Flyers Cups are a record unrivalled in the state. The school's recipe for success is a mix of Tier 1 and Tier 2 players who compete against the best in the northeastern United States throughout the year prior to the playoffs. LaSalle has arguably been the most dominant high school hockey program at any level in Pennsylvania since bursting on the scene in 1996 under Muehlbronner. The Explorers have won six state titles and 10 Flyers Cups in that time and have been a part of the Flyers Cup finals for a majority of that period. There is no question that this program will continue to leave its mark on state history and could surpass Meadville in the very near future. (Both, courtesy of LaSalle College Prep Hockey.)

John Graves is a native of Philadelphia and has contributed greatly to the game of hockey at all levels, with the creation and operation of the Ice Line facility in West Chester. He started coaching at Malvern Prep in 1997 and put together an impressive run in Eastern Pennsylvania, including state championships in 2004 and six Flyers Cup wins (1997, 2001–2005). Father Ed Casey was with Graves for 10 years at Malvern Prep. The Friars had an impressive 25-9-0 record in the playoffs and were the bridesmaid four of five years from 2001 through 2005, falling to Bethel Park in four one-goal games along the way. Malvern Prep was the dominant high school hockey program at the AAA level in the state from 1997 to 2005, with six Flyers Cups and one state title in 2004. The Achilles heel for the Friars was that they faced Bethel Park in 1997, 2001, 2002, and 2005, and Meadville in 2003, losing by one goal each time. Malvern Prep was a Flyers Cup juggernaut, losing only nine times in ten years, with five of those in the state finals. Many of John Graves's players moved on to play Division I and Division III hockey at the NCAA level. (Courtesy of Malvern Prep Hockey.)

Peters Township burst onto the high school hockey scene in 2002. Mark Cooper's seven years at the helm were productive, as the Indians won three state championships (2002, 2003, 2005) and four consecutive Penguins Cup championships (2002–2005). Rick Tingle took over in 2006 and has continued the tradition of excellence, adding two state championships in 2014 and 2017, to bring the total number of state titles to six. Scott Simmons was the assistant coach for Mark Cooper, and Cliff Bumford has been with Rick Tingle for a majority of his 15 years at Peters Township. The record for Peters Township hockey over this 20-year run is impressive, at 332-121-22, and 45-14 in the playoffs. Cooper's record in six years was 117-30-3, including a 20-3 mark in the playoffs. Tingle has tallied a record of 215-91-19 and 25-11 in the playoffs. Peters Township's program has been based upon terrific numbers in development within the club who compete for their high school teams and at a very good amateur level at both Tier 1 and Tier 2. Peters The Indians ran the table in the 2002 Penguins Cup and throttled Archbishop Carroll in the state finals. This led to four consecutive Penguins Cups and three state titles under Cooper. The program continued to grow in numbers and talent, and from 2010 to 2019 reached the Penguins Cup finals seven times in nine years, netting two state titles and two Penguins Cups, to rank among the elite programs in Class AAA in Pennsylvania. (Courtesy of the Pennsylvania Hockey Foundation Archives.)

Nine

TOP 50 PACE SETTERS AND LEGENDARY PLAYERS

Over 45 years of the Pennsylvania high school hockey championships, there have been many great teams coached by terrific coaches. The championships have yielded some great performances. But it is the players who take the ice who decide their destiny. In this list of the top 50 players who left their mark on the state championships, there are players who won multiple titles, provided overtime heroics, scored hat tricks, had a dominant performance, or continued their careers in NCAA or professional hockey. (Keep in mind that this list is exclusive to the state championships.) Each and every player who made the cut is to be commended. The school size or level of play did not matter. Imagine the best players from the pioneer days of hockey competing against the leading talents from today. What an exciting game that would be. (Courtesy of the Pennsylvania Hockey Foundation Archives.)

To win a state championship is a dream realized, and the group of players who have won multiple titles is a very rare group. Bayard Rustin's Jason Grande and Matt Owens, Bishop McCort's Kris Carlson, and Meadville's Scott Phillis headline a group who won four consecutive crowns. Joining them with near-perfect careers was Meadville's Ryan Smart and Bishop McCort's Brett Houston as three-time winners. (Courtesy of Meadville Bulldog Hockey.)

Radnor's John and Chris Brennan and Quaker Valley's Colin and Furman South headline the dominant brothers who join this list and led their schools to multiple final appearances. (Courtesy of Bayard Rustin Hockey.)

Players with multiple state championship appearances are Monsignor Bonner's Jerry DiStefano, Germantown Academy's Rob Shaner, and Downingtown East's Luca Pisani. (Courtesy of Furman South.)

Great performances in the state finals have provided some great memories, but winning in overtime just adds to the lore of many players in this group. Baldwin's Jim Cox won the very first state title in overtime in 1975 and was joined a year later by Abington's Dennis Garvin. Joining these titans with memorable goals in overtime are West Chester's Doug Bowman in 1982, Conwell Egan's Brian Tetley in 1999, Bethel Park's Justin Glock in 2001, and Bayard Rustin's Matt Owens in 2017. (Courtesy of Bethel Park Hockey.)

Not to be outdone are players who dominated the state finals by scoring hat tricks or more to lead their schools to victory. Canevin's Greg Timmons registered hat tricks in the 1983 and 1984 title games. Chartiers Valley's Tim Tracy notched four goals in the 1986 final. Council Rock's Roman Bussetti scored a hat trick to help Council Rock in its first state title in 1991. In 1993 and 1994, Greensburg Central Catholic's Jeff Adams scored four times. Quaker Valley standout Furman South scored four times in the 2006 final. (Above, courtesy of EPIHA; left, courtesy of Jeff Adams.)

The list of Pennsylvanians who moved on to play at a higher level after high school is a who's who of state hockey. Gateway's John Liprando moved on to Denver University. Upper St. Clair's Bobby Kennedy went on to play at Bowling Green. Scott Chamness led Archbishop Carroll to the Flyers Cup in 1980 and moved on to St. Lawrence University. Malvern Prep's Keith Grimley moved on to play at the University of Connecticut. Bethel Park's Keith Stanich went to Wayne State, and Seton LaSalle's Lou Garritan forged an NCAA career at Bemidji State University. (Right, courtesy of Seton LaSalle Hockey; below, courtesy of Furman South.)

Malvern Prep's Chris Lawrence went on to play for Michigan State and in a national championship. Peters Township's Matt Clackson played in the NCAA at Western Michigan. Holy Ghost Prep's Ryan Gunderson played for Vermont and represented the United States in the Olympics. Peters Township's Rob Madore also headed to Vermont. Germantown Academy's Brian O'Neill excelled at Yale and played in the Olympics. Mt. Lebanon's Tyler Murovich played in the Ontario Hockey League. North Allegheny's Wes Waldschmidt led Slippery Rock to the ACHA nationals and became that league's all-time leading scorer. Bayard Rustin's Eric Knodel played in the American Hockey League. (Courtesy of Mike Ivcic.)

West Chester Henderson's Billy Latta went on to play at the University of Connecticut. LaSalle's Adam Berkle played at Bowling Green. Bayard Rustin's Brian Christie played at Merrimack. Cardinal O'Hara's Ricky DeRosa played at Penn State. LaSalle tandem Nick Master and Andrew Romano both played at the University of Massachusetts–Lowell. Latrobe's Dalton Hunter moved on to the NCAA at Mercyhurst. (Courtesy of PIHL.)

Finally, for those kids who aspire to play in the National Hockey League, these Pennsylvanians played high school hockey and succeeded. Thomas Jefferson's John Zeiler played for Los Angeles, Peters Township's Christian Hanson played for Toronto, and Mt. Lebanon's Matt Bartkowski played for Boston and Calgary; all won the state championship. Germantown Academy won its first state title in 1983, with Mike Ritcher moving on to the University of Wisconsin and then to the Rangers, winning a Stanley Cup in 1994. Brandon Saad did not have a memorable state final in 2008 for Pine Richland as a freshman but rebounded to play in the Ontario Hockey League and National Hockey League with Chicago, winning the Stanley Cup twice. (Above, courtesy of Chicago Blackhawks; below, courtesy of New York Rangers.)

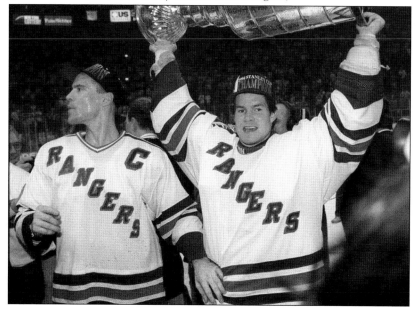

Pennsylvania
State Champions

Year	State AAA Champion	State AA Champion	State A Champion
1975	Baldwin (WPIHL)		
1976	Mt. Lebanon (WPIHL)	Abington (ICSCHL)	
1977	Churchill (WPIHL)	Erie Fairview (LKSHL)	
1978			
1979	Churchill (WPIHL)	South Hills Catholic (WPIHL)	
1980	Upper St. Clair (SHIHL)		
1981	Archbishop Carroll (ICSCHL)	Erie Fairview (LKSHL)	
1982	West Chester (ICSCHL)	Erie Fairview (LKSHL)	
1983	Germantown Academy (SHSHL)	Canevin (SHIHL)	
1984	Cathedral Prep (LKSHL)	Canevin (SHIHL)	
1985	Conestoga (ICSCHL)	Pennsbury (LBCSHL)	
1986	Conestoga (ICSCHL)	Chartiers Valley (SHIHL)	
1987	Upper St. Clair (SHIHL)	Meadville (LKSHL)	
1988	Baldwin (SHIHL)	William Tennent (SHSHL)	
1989	Meadville (LKSHL)	Canevin (SHIHL)	Plum (WPIHL)
1990	Malvern Prep (ICSHL)	Father Judge (LBCSHL)	Bishop Egan (LBCSHL)
1991	Council Rock (SHSHL)	Beaver (SHIHL)	Monsignor Bonner (EHSHL)
1992	Meadville (LKSHL)	Council Rock (SHSHL)	Haverford (EHSHL)
1993	Meadville (LKSHL)	Father Judge (LBCSHL)	Greensburg CC (WPIHL)
1994	Meadville (LKSHL)	Greensburg CC (WPIHL)	Bishop McCort (WPIHL)

Year	State AAA Champion	State AA Champion	State A Champion
1995	Meadville (LKSHL)	Conwell Egan (LBCSHL)	Bishop McCort (WPIHL)
1996	Meadville (LKSHL)	Greensburg CC (WPIHL)	Bishop McCort (WPIHL)
1997	Bethel Park (SHIHL)	Cathedral Prep (LKSHL)	Bishop McCort (WPIHL)
1998	Lasalle (ICSCHL)	Thomas Jefferson (SHIHL)	Seton Lasalle (SHIHL)
1999	Conwell Egan (LBCSHL)	Thomas Jefferson (SHIHL)	Bishop McCort (WPIHL)
2000	Bethel Park (PIHL)	Thomas Jefferson (SHIHL)	Serra Catholic (PIHL)
2001	Bethel Park (PIHL)	Beaver (PIHL)	Serra Catholic (PIHL)
2002	Bethel Park (PIHL)	Peters Township (PIHL)	Serra Catholic (PIHL)
2003	Meadville (PIHL)	Peters Township (PIHL)	Radnor (ICSCHL)
2004	Malvern Prep (ICSCHL)	Archbishop Carroll (ICSCHL)	Radnor (ICSCHL)
2005	Bethel Park (PIHL)	Peters Township (PIHL)	Penncrest (ICSCHL)
2006	Mt. Lebanon (PIHL)	Pine Richland (PIHL)	Quaker Valley (PIHL)
2007	North Allegheny (PIHL)	Pine Richland (PIHL)	West Chester Henderson (ICSCHL)
2008	Lasalle (ICSCHL)	Latrobe (PIHL)	West Chester East (ICSCHL)
2009	Lasalle (ICSCHL)	Latrobe (PIHL)	Bayard Rustin (ICSCHL)
2010	Cardinal O'Hara (EHSHL)	Latrobe (PIHL)	Mars (PIHL)
2011	Upper St. Clair (PIHL)	Canevin (PIHL)	Mars (PIHL)
2012	Lasalle (ICSCHL)	Council Rock South (SHSHL)	Quaker Valley (PIHL)
2013	North Allegheny (PIHL)	Latrobe (PIHL)	West Chester East (ICSCHL)
2014	Peters Township (PIHL)	Central Bucks South (SHSHL)	Bayard Rustin (ICSCHL)
2015	Holy Ghost Prep (ICSCHL)	Cathedral Prep (PIHL)	Bayard Rustin (ICSCHL)
2016	Lasalle (ICSCHL)	Central Bucks South (SHSHL)	Bayard Rustin (ICSCHL)
2017	Peters Township (PIHL)	Downingtown East (ICSCHL)	Bayard Rustin (ICSCHL)
2018	St. Joseph's Prep (ICSCHL)	Downingtown East (ICSCHL)	Bayard Rustin (ICSCHL)
2019	Lasalle (ICSCHL)	Pine Richland (PIHL)	Bayard Rustin (ICSCHL)

PENGUINS CUP WESTERN CHAMPIONS

Year	AAA Champion	AA Champion	A Champion
1975	Baldwin (WPIHL)		
1976	Mt. Lebanon (WPIHL)	Gateway (WPIHL)	
1977	Churchill (WPIHL)	Erie Fairview (LKSHL)	
1978			
1979	Churchill (WPIHL)	South Hills Catholic (WPIHL)	
1980	Upper St. Clair (SHIHL)		
1981	North Catholic (WPIHL)	Erie Fairview (LKSHL)	
1982	Baldwin (SHIHL)	Erie Fairview (LKSHL)	
1983	Bethel Park (SHIHL)	Canevin (SHIHL)	
1984	Erie Cathedral Prep (LKSHL)	Canevin (SHIHL)	
1985	Mt. Lebanon (SHIHL)	Canevin (SHIHL)	
1986	Upper St. Clair (SHIHL)	Chartiers Valley (SHIHL)	
1987	Upper St. Clair (SHIHL)	Meadville (LKSHL)	
1988	Baldwin (SHIHL)	Allderdice (WPIHL)	
1989	Meadville (LKSHL)	Canevin (SHIHL)	Plum (WPIHL)
1990	Upper St. Clair (SHIHL)	Johnstown (WPIHL)	Ringgold (SHIHL)
1991	Armstrong Central (WPIHL)	Beaver (SHIHL)	State College (LKSHL)
1992	Meadville (LKSHL)	Johnstown (WPIHL)	Greensburg CC (WPIHL)
1993	Meadville (LKSHL)	Canevin (SHIHL)	Greensburg CC (WPIHL)
1994	Meadville (LKSHL)	Greensburg CC (WPIHL)	Bishop McCort (WPIHL)
1995	Meadville (LKSHL)	North Catholic (WPIHL)	Bishop McCort (WPIHL)

Year	AAA Champion	AA Champion	A Champion
1996	Meadville (LKSHL)	Greensburg CC (WPIHL)	Bishop McCort (WPIHL)
1997	Bethel Park (SHIHL)	Cathedral Prep (LKSHL)	Bishop McCort (WPIHL)
1998	Central Catholic (WPIHL)	Thomas Jefferson (SHIHL)	Seton Lasalle (SHIHL)
1999	Meadville (LKSHL)	Thomas Jefferson (SHIHL)	Bishop McCort (WPIHL)
2000	Bethel Park (PIHL)	Thomas Jefferson (PIHL)	Serra Catholic (PIHL)
2001	Bethel Park (PIHL)	Beaver (PIHL)	Serra Catholic (PIHL)
2002	Bethel Park (PIHL)	Peters Township (PIHL)	Serra Catholic (PIHL)
2003	Meadville (PIHL)	Peters Township (PIHL)	Westmont Hilltop (PIHL)
2004	Mt. Lebanon (PIHL)	Peters Township (PIHL)	Serra Catholic (PIHL)
2005	Bethel Park (PIHL)	Peters Township (PIHL)	Bishop McCort (PIHL)
2006	Mt. Lebanon (PIHL)	Pine Richland (PIHL)	Quaker Valley (PIHL)
2007	North Allegheny (PIHL)	Pine Richland (PIHL)	Freeport (PIHL)
2008	Pine Richland (PIHL)	Latrobe (PIHL)	Quaker Valley (PIHL)
2009	Shaler (PIHL)	Latrobe (PIHL)	Mars (PIHL)
2010	Canon McMillan (PIHL)	Latrobe (PIHL)	Mars (PIHL)
2011	Upper St. Clair (PIHL)	Canevin (PIHL)	Mars (PIHL)
2012	Bethel Park (PIHL)	West Allegheny (PIHL)	Quaker Valley (PIHL)
2013	North Allegheny (PIHL)	Latrobe (PIHL)	Quaker Valley (PIHL)
2014	Peters Township (PIHL)	Canevin (PIHL)	Quaker Valley (PIHL)
2015	Canon McMillan (PIHL)	Cathedral Prep (PIHL)	Mars (PIHL)
2016	Cathedral Prep (PIHL)	Canevin (PIHL)	Franklin Regional (PIHL)
2017	Peters Township (PIHL)	Plum (PIHL)	Franklin Regional (PIHL)
2018	Seneca Valley (PIHL)	Armstrong (PIHL)	Bishop McCort (PIHL)
2019	North Allegheny (PIHL)	Pine Richland (PIHL)	Montour (PIHL)

FLYERS CUP
EASTERN CHAMPIONS

Year	AAA Champion	AA Champion	A Champion
1980	Archbishop Carroll (ICSCHL)		
1981	Archbishop Carroll (ICSCHL)		
1982	Germantown Academy (SHSHL)		
1983	Germantown Academy (SHSHL)		
1984	Archbishop Ryan (LBCSHL)		
1985	Cherry Hill East (SHSHL)		
1986	Conestoga (ICSCHL)		
1987	Malvern Prep (EHSHL)		
1988	Council Rock (SHSHL)		
1989	William Tennent (NHSHL)		
1990	Malvern Prep (EHSHL)		
1991	Council Rock (SHSHL)	Germantown Academy (SHSHL)	Monsignor Bonner (EHSHL)
1992	Monsignor Bonner (EHSHL)	Council Rock (SHSHL)	Haverford (EHSHL)
1993	Monsignor Bonner (EHSHL)	Father Judge (LBCSHL)	Pennsbury (LBCSHL)
1994	Germantown Academy (SHSHL)	Conwell-Egan (LBCSHL)	Washington Township (SJHSHL)
1995	Germantown Academy (SHSHL)	Conwell-Egan (LBCSHL)	Unionville (ICSHL)
1996	Lasalle (ICSCHL)	Upper Darby (EHSHL)	St. Pius X (ICSCHL)
1997	Malvern Prep (ICSCHL)	Conestoga (ICSCHL)	Marple-Newtown (EHSHL)
1998	Lasalle (ICSCHL)	Unionville (ICSCHL)	Garnet Valley (ICSCHL)

Year	AAA Champion	AA Champion	A Champion
1999	Conwell-Egan (LBCSHL)	Lasalle II (ICSCHL)	Archbishop Ryan (LBCSHL)
2000	Father Judge (LBCSHL)	Archbishop Carroll (ICSCHL)	Pennsbury (LBCSHL)
2001	Malvern Prep (ICSCHL)	Archbishop Carroll (ICSCHL)	Springfield (EHSHL)
2002	Malvern Prep (ICSCHL)	Archbishop Carroll (ICSCHL)	Radnor (ICSCHL)
2003	Malvern Prep (ICSCHL)	Holy Ghost Prep (LBCSHL)	Radnor (ICSCHL)
2004	Malvern Prep (ICSCHL)	Archbishop Carroll (ICSCHL)	Radnor (ICSCHL)
2005	Malvern Prep (ICSCHL)	Haverford (EHSHL)	Penncrest (ICSCHL)
2006	Cardinal O'Hara (EHSHL)	Haverford (EHSHL)	Penncrest (ICSCHL)
2007	Holy Ghost Prep (LBCSHL)	Haverford (EHSHL)	West Chester Henderson (ICSCHL)
2008	Lasalle (ICSCHL)	Conestoga (ICSCHL)	West Chester East (ICSCHL)
2009	Lasalle (ICSCHL)	Council Rock South (SHSHL)	Bayard Rustin (ICSCHL)
2010	Cardinal O'Hara (ICSCHL)	Downingtown East (ICSCHL)	Bayard Rustin (ICSCHL)
2011	Lasalle (ICSCHL)	Council Rock South (SHSHL)	Springfield (ICSCHL)
2012	Lasalle (ICSCHL)	Council Rock South (SHSHL)	Bayard Rustin (ICSCHL)
2013	Lasalle (ICSCHL)	Cherokee (SJSHL)	West Chester East (ICSCHL)
2014	Lasalle (ICSCHL)	Central Bucks South (SHSHL)	Bayard Rustin (ICSCHL)
2015	Holy Ghost Prep (ICSCHL)	Downingtown East (ICSCHL)	Bayard Rustin (ICSCHL)
2016	Lasalle (ICSCHL)	Central Bucks South (SHSHL)	Bayard Rustin (ICSCHL)
2017	Holy Ghost Prep (ICSCHL)	Downingtown East (ICSCHL)	Bayard Rustin (ICSCHL)
2018	St. Joseph's Prep (ICSCHL)	Downingtown East (ICSCHL)	Bayard Rustin (ICSCHL)
2019	Lasalle (ICSCHL)	Downingtown East (ICSCHL)	Bayard Rustin (ICSCHL)

DISCOVER THOUSANDS OF LOCAL HISTORY BOOKS
FEATURING MILLIONS OF VINTAGE IMAGES

Arcadia Publishing, the leading local history publisher in the United States, is committed to making history accessible and meaningful through publishing books that celebrate and preserve the heritage of America's people and places.

Find more books like this at
www.arcadiapublishing.com

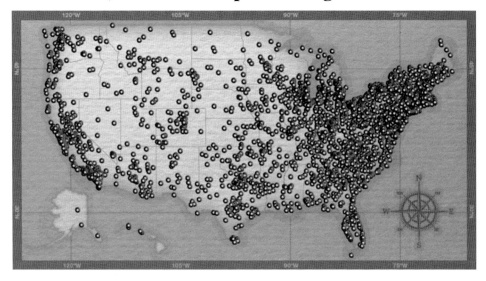

Search for your hometown history, your old stomping grounds, and even your favorite sports team.